# WHAT DO YOU SAY WHEN…

# WHAT DO YOU SAY WHEN...

## AN INSPIRATIONAL GUIDE TO WITNESSING

### NELLIE PICKARD

Foreword by Joseph M. Stowell

**BAKER BOOK HOUSE**
Grand Rapids, Michigan 49506

ISBN: 0-8010-7106-2

Printed in the United States of America

Scripture quotations are taken from the Holy Bible, New International
Version. Copyright © 1973, 1978, 1984 International Bible Society. Used
by permission of Zondervan Bible Publishers.


**Library of Congress Cataloging-in-Publication Data**

Pickard, Nellie.
      What do you say when—.

      1. Witness bearing (Christianity)    2. Evangelistic
work.    I. Title.
BV4520.P5    1988              248'.5              88-22284
ISBN 0-8010-7106-2

To my beloved husband
**Paul,**
whose life desire is to live Ephesians 5:25
"Husbands love your wives
just as Christ loved the church
and gave Himself up for her."
Because of his encouragement
this book was completed.

# Contents

Foreword    9
Preface    11
Acknowledgments    15
Introduction    17

**What to Say When . . .**

1. She Says, "But I Wasn't Predestined to
   Have Such Faith"    25
2. A Stranger Says, "Aren't You a Sight!"    30
3. Someone Asks About "Earning" the Right
   to Witness    34
4. A Young Woman Says, "My Life Is Such a Mess.
   I Just Want to End It All"    38
5. Your Neighbors Think You Spend Your Time
   Passing Judgment on Them    46
6. She Says, "Having Just Had a Brush With Death,
   My Thinking About Life Has Changed"    51
7. A Neighbor Says, "I'd Like to Talk to You—But
   I'm Just Not Ready Yet"    60
8. A Stranger Asks If He Can Hug You    63
9. She Says, "I Know All That. It's Not Going to
   Help Me Any!"    67
10. She Says, "It Really Doesn't Matter What You
    Believe, as Long as You're Sincere"    73

11. A Shopper Admires a Nightshirt That Says,
    "When I'm Sleeping, I'm a Saint"    84
12. The Tennis Pro Says, "I Attend Church Only at
    Christmas and Easter"    89
13. A Jewish Man Asks If You Resent His People
    Because They Did Not Accept Christ
    as Messiah    93
14. Someone Seems Happy in a Cultist Church    98
15. A Young Man Says, "I'm Really Depressed About
    My Life"    103
16. She Says, "I Think I'm Going Crazy!"    107
17. Someone Asks, "What Do You Think About
    Homosexuals?"    113
18. She Says, "I Wish I Knew God Better"    120
19. They Say, "We Don't Get Much out of Church.
    It Seems Dull and Boring"    124
20. He Says, "We Live Together; I Like to Try the
    Merchandise Before I Buy"    131
21. She Says, "My Family Didn't Place Much
    Importance on Jesus Christ"    134
22. He Says, "We Won't Have Peace Until Messiah
    Comes"    138
23. She Says, "I'm a Very Confused Person. They Tell
    Me I'm Manic Depressive"    142
24. She Says, "I Have a Problem—I Don't Know How
    to Pray"    150
25. She Says, "I'm Searching . . . but I Don't Think
    I've Found Him Yet"    157
26. She Says, "Shut Up!"    161
27. She Says, "I Just Can't Understand a God Who
    Would Take an Innocent Child's Life"    170
28. He Says, "I'm Beyond Redemption"    176
29. The Holy Spirit Has Already Worked    185
30. Others Want to Know Him, Too    189

# Foreword

During baseball season, televised games are interrupted by spectacular moments of baseball history. They capture the thrill and essence of America's favorite pastime. As the promo draws to a close, the words blaze across the screen, "Baseball Fever . . . Catch It."

Nellie Pickard has a certain fever for evangelism, and those of us who enjoy her friendship have found it contagious. Evangelism is indeed more caught than taught. My own witness for Christ has been stimulated by the author's creative approach to loving the lost. For her, evangelism is not a project; it is a passion. The lost that she encounters are for her an opportunity to express the life-changing love of Christ.

You will be intrigued, challenged, encouraged, instructed, and enabled after reading these glimpses of the power of God unto salvation. Nellie Pickard's effective use of personal encounter will open new vistas of awareness and sensitivity.

I am delighted that you are reading this book. The

author reinforces my prejudice that true evangelism comes from the overflow of a loving, gracious heart. I am delighted, as well, for the sake of the gospel.

While some will not be able to relate to others exactly as Nellie does, since she is the ultimate people-person, these episodes will teach us to see others in terms of their need and the precious gift of Christ.

While effective evangelism is done in many different ways, this book will add an important arrow to your quiver. *Catch it!*

Joseph M. Stowell
President, Moody Bible Institute

# Preface

Another book on witnessing? Why?

"Nellie, do you believe people have to verbalize their witness? Don't you think their lifestyle should be their witness?" One of my friends stopped me with these questions.

I answered, "If our lives contradict what we say, our witness will not be effective; but no matter how perfect a life we live, no one will ever know the way to become a Christian unless we tell them."

People often say to me, "I wish I had witnessed to the person I spoke to today. I had a perfect opportunity but I didn't know what to say." Then they go around feeling guilty because they didn't speak up for the Lord. These opportunities are not mere coincidences but God's divine appointments.

I hope that by eavesdropping on my stories the reader will feel more relaxed about saying a word here or there and truly enjoy obeying the Lord's command to "Be my witnesses," whether it be sowing the seed, watering or reaping. Only God can give the increase.

11

I am an ordinary Michigan homemaker (with a husband, Paul; two daughters and a son, all married; and eight grandchildren) who likes to play tennis and swim, cook, and have company.

God has given me a love for himself (and this is the most important part of my life), a love for his Word, and a love for his children—and he has used me to lead many people to trust in Christ as their Savior. Day by day, the Lord teaches me his Word and ministers to me as I study it. I look for principles to remember and live by and make it a habit to share what I find so that, as I tell others, these principles become more a part of me. I pray for opportunities to tell what I have learned to people who do not know the Lord. I love to spread the Good News!

I read Scripture with care and listen attentively when being taught the Word by another. As I listen, I jot down phrases the speaker uses so that later, when I am studying my notes, the message comes back clearly—just as it was delivered. Then I ask the Holy Spirit to apply the truth of the Word to my life.

I ask God for grace and strength as I face temptation, and I make it a habit to keep short accounts with God. I confess my sin to the One who is faithful and just to forgive my sin and to cleanse me from all unrighteousness. And then I am free to witness with strength and boldness. I can speak up because I am not crippled by sin and guilt. Christ is my righteousness. Because I am at peace in my own heart, I have no reason to fear other people. Everything's all right here at home.

How does the Lord give me a love for others? The first fruit of the Holy Spirit is "love." Christ prayed to the Father that "the love you have for me may be in them and that I myself may be in them" (John 17:26). The

Father's love is in me because Christ is in me. My responsibility is to let him "love the world" (to use John 3:16 language) through me.

How does the Lord nudge me when it's time to speak? First, I listen carefully when conversing with people, since I know from Scripture that God wants me to be sensitive to the needs of others, whether those needs are spiritual, emotional, or physical. I pray for that sensitivity and keep alert for openings to speak about the Lord, so witnessing is as natural for me as eating and drinking. When I see a "chocolate-covered cookie," I go for it. When certain things are said to me, my spiritual radar rings in my ear. The Holy Spirit gives me a nudge. I follow the opening in the conversation and speak up for the Lord.

I recently moved into a new neighborhood. Naturally, I wanted to get to know people. When someone asked me to be a delegate for a political party and collect the signatures of twenty people, I took the opportunity. I went door to door—in this case using politics as my opening—and got acquainted with twenty new people, all neighbors. Now I have an occasion to build on those encounters, to be wise and sensitive and giving, to relax and let the Holy Spirit lead conversations about the changing political scene into conversations about an unchanging Savior and his love.

When I was a girl, I went to all the meetings led by Dr. Walter L. Wilson when he spoke in my city. He was a soulwinner, and he gave all the details of his witnessing experiences—what he said and what the other person said and then what he said in response. We in the congregation were able to relive his experiences. I found this immensely profitable. It took all the mystery out of witnessing. Dr. Wilson made it as practical as washing dishes, but so much more vital.

That is exactly what I want to do in this little book. I want to share incidents when the Holy Spirit gave me a nudge as I have talked with everyday people. I want to tell what they said and what I said. I want to show how naturally our conversations got started, and I want you to see how spiritual things were brought in. At the end of each story, I want to reflect back and emphasize a learning experience and perhaps press a particular point home.

In the process, Lord willing, I want to take the mystique out of soulwinning.

Then, I trust, the Holy Spirit will give *you* the nudge to try it, too.

# Acknowledgments

I am deeply indebted to Connie Gonser, historical writer for the Royal Oak, Michigan, public school system, for her initial encouragement and continuing support. She spent many evenings in my home reading my stories and urging me to keep on writing.

I want to thank my many friends who prayed me through this project.

I am deeply indebted and immensely grateful to Dick Bohrer, my teacher at the Maranatha Writers' Conference. After reading part of my manuscript, he wrote to me and said, "I believe in your stories. I will help you all I can." Dick has an unusual ability to inspire. He guided me but never put words in my mouth. "The book has to be you," he would say over and over again. He made me believe I could write. I finally believed him, and thus this book. He not only edited my work but also gave me many suggestions. Despite his many responsibilities, he was never too busy to talk to me on the phone. His editing was invaluable.

I thank God for the Dick Bohrers in this world.

# Introduction

First, I would like to tell you how I got started in witnessing. . . .

I will always be grateful to my parents for the Bible teaching I had in my home and in my church during my early years. I grew up knowing what the Bible said about such things as behavior, and it was this that made me uneasy every time I did something sneaky. The things I did—like skipping church with a friend or spending my collection money at the corner drug store—may seem insignificant to others, but they weighed heavily on my conscience. Instead of enjoying my "freedom," I felt miserable.

Now, I didn't do these things too often—just once in a while, when I thought I wouldn't get caught. What I learned in church was mostly in my head. Though I even memorized many portions of Scripture, reading the Bible then was like reading a history book. I believed it, but it had little effect on my life. You might say I was brain-washed but not heart-washed.

I had an excellent environment—a church where the

Bible was taught as the Word of God and parents who loved me and honored the Lord. In some ways I was badly spoiled with the good things of Christianity. I was like a child surrounded by wealth but preferring to live like a pauper. It took a while before the message of salvation became a reality in my heart. In the meantime, I enjoyed life with my friends because their lifestyle was pretty much like my own.

For the most part, I was a bit like my three-year-old grandson, Reuben. We had had a big day at the beach—he and I. We made sand castles, played at the edge of the ocean, letting the waves come at us. We went to McDonald's and played on the swings and slides. When we got home, I was tired and went to my room. It wasn't long before I heard a knock at my door.

"May I come in, Gramma?"

"Sure, Reuben."

"Watcha doing, Gramma?"

"Oh, reading and relaxing a bit."

"Mom's going to read me a story, too," he said as he came toward me.

He put his two little hands on my cheeks and gave me a kiss. "Goodnight, Gramma." Then he left the room.

*How sweet*, I thought. *What a wonderful child. Everyone should have a child like that.*

Then I heard him call to his mother. "I did what you told me to, Mom." That kiss wasn't so great after all—but he did as he was told.

As a child, I was like that. I loved the Lord pretty much as I was told. It wasn't popular to rebel in those days—at least, not outwardly. I just pretended to be an obedient young lady.

One night, as my parents and I arrived at church, I announced to them that I didn't feel up to staying for the evening service and that I would like to go home and rest. My parents trusted me and sent me on my way.

Enroute, I met one of my friends and suggested she come home and have a bite to eat with me. Then a couple of boys we knew came along. They were hungry, too. Though I never had people over without my parents' permission—especially boys—we were all hungry, so we went to my house.

At first, it seemed exciting and daring to have boys at my house when my parents weren't there. Then I began to feel uneasy. I don't remember how it got started, but one of the boys began to get a little too friendly. I got them to leave by telling them my folks would be coming home any minute and was greatly relieved when they were gone. It was a close call, but it was one of the experiences in my life that added to the guilt that kept piling up.

No one needed to convince me that, when the Bible said all have sinned and come short of God's ideal, it was true. I knew all my friends sinned. I saw them do it every day. Some of them were mean and selfish; others were critical and catty. Then, one day, I discovered that it wasn't just my friends who had a sin problem. I did, too.

One night I responded to the minister's invitation to accept Christ as my Savior. He was explaining that Jesus, being God in the flesh, had come to earth to seek and to save the lost. It was then that I realized that my friends and I were not the only ones with a sin problem. It was epidemic. It was worldwide. The whole world had sinned and stood guilty before God. No one could reach God's standard.

My heart was moved when I began to understand through Scripture that Christ came for the very purpose of dying on the cross for *my* sin. In fact, he died in my place, as my substitute. He who knew no sin became sin—for me.

This was an overwhelming truth. How could it be? I didn't deserve it. Then I understood that it was a gift. Salvation was a gift I received by putting my faith in Jesus Christ. I couldn't work for it. All I needed to do was to accept him, receive him, choose him—however you want to say it—and I did.

Then, through the Scriptures, I learned another wonderful truth. It was that not only did Jesus Christ die for my sins, but he also rose from the dead and is alive today. And because he arose, I will arise and be with him in heaven when I die. That was tremendous security. As though that was not enough, I also discovered that since the Lord Jesus lives in me through the Holy Spirit, I am never alone.

That night, by receiving Christ as my Savior, I was born into the family of God.

Some years later, I met and fell in love with Paul. He was a committed Christian and had his priorities straight: God was first in his life and home. We married two years after our first date. We had three children, two girls—Karen and Greta—and a boy—Tim. They are married now, and Paul and I have eight grandchildren.

I wish I could say that I stayed close to the Lord all of my married life. I experienced some growing pains, or perhaps I should say that I suffered some spiritual malnutrition. I neglected my spiritual food (my Bible reading) because of the business and cares of daily life.

When the children were small, my mother died and my father came to live with us. This was not easy for him or for us. He missed my mother greatly and demanded much of my time. My children needed me, and my husband was working ten and twelve hours a day. I felt fragmented and became impatient and irritable. I should have known where to go for my strength, but I tried to work it out my own way. I fell flat on my face and felt like a failure.

Then God did something special. Our church held a seminar that lasted five evenings. The idea was to help us articulate the gospel so that we could be witnessing Christians. My husband and I decided to attend.

The first night, they gave us an assignment, and I thought it was a strange one. "Go home," they said, "and ask the Lord to show you if there is anything in your life that displeases him. When he shows you, confess it." That's all there was to the assignment.

I went home thinking, *There's nothing wrong with my life.* After all, wasn't I taking care of my father, and wasn't I a good mother and wasn't I a good wife—and wasn't I this and wasn't I that?

Since I wanted to cooperate, I prayed rather self-righteously: "Lord, would you please show me if there is anything in my life that displeases you?"

I think I must have expected to hear, "Well done, thou good and faithful servant." But I didn't. It wasn't long before I realized I was being a bit self-righteous. I had tried to work out my problem in my own strength—I hadn't asked for guidance or strength from the Lord. Something else came to my mind that I wanted to push away, though it wouldn't leave.

I had recently gone shopping and had seen an item I wanted. It was expensive, and I knew I should first discuss it with my husband. You see, we had decided that anything over $25.00 should not be purchased without first talking it over with each other. Money was a bit tight in those days, and it really was a good rule.

21

The more I looked at this item (to this day, I can't remember what it was—so it couldn't have been very important), the more I wanted it. So I bought it, thinking, *What Paul doesn't know won't hurt him.*

It did hurt, but not him. It hurt *me* because, when God put his finger on that sin, I realized that I had not been honest. I confessed it to the Lord and felt peace. I then had to confess it to my husband.

"Paul," I said, "I bought something last week that I should not have bought. It was too expensive. I knew better, but I bought it anyway. I'm sorry."

In a very loving voice, he said, "Well, honey, if you think it's worth it, that's fine."

"No, it's not fine. I was deliberately deceitful and I'm truly sorry. I ask your forgiveness."

Paul forgave me and we prayed together.

There were many things wrong in my life at that time, but God did not overwhelm me with my shortcomings all at once. He just started pecking away—and he still does. As I said before, I want to keep short accounts with him.

I am sharing these things because I believe that known sin in a person's life is a hindrance to effective witnessing. That experience was a new step of growth in my life. In fact, life has been an adventure ever since.

The second assignment, the next night of the seminar, was: "If you have made things right with God, then tell him you are available to him."

I liked that because it took all the pressure out of witnessing. So I said to the Lord, "I'd like to be available to you. Just show me the people you want me to witness to." I didn't know how it would work, but I committed myself to being available to him for the rest of my life.

The next morning I thought I had better get started

on my Christmas shopping. Before I left home, I had my quiet time with the Lord. I reminded him that I wanted to be available to him. Though I knew that he didn't need reminding, I mentioned it in my prayer to remind myself.

I started my day with an air of expectancy, but I was also a bit afraid that God would take me up on my offer. I can say now that it was an exciting day, because it was the day I met Mary and discovered how wonderfully natural it seemed to witness for the Lord.

# 1

## What To Say When . . .

### *She Says, "But I Wasn't Predestined to Have Such Faith"*

**Mary**

A new mall had just opened, and I was eager to take advantage of the bargains. It was Christmastime and the window section of one of the stores was beautifully decorated. The manger scene with angels hovering above was the main attraction. I enjoyed looking at all the details and listening to the carols being sung.

*I wonder if the people are hearing the words,* I thought.

I was grateful to the management for the beautiful music and mentioned this fact to several of the sales persons and to the manager. Then I noticed that little round tables for two were set up and that free coffee and cookies were being served, so I sat down to enjoy the holiday atmosphere.

As I looked around, I noticed a woman loaded down with packages. She seemed very tired and dejected and was looking for a place to sit. I gave her a big smile and motioned for her to come and sit with me.

She seemed relieved and sighed heavily. "Oh, me, I sure don't have the spirit of Christmas. Do you?"

"What's your problem?" I asked.

"Well, my son isn't going to be home for Christmas. Life changes so much when the children leave home. Christmas this year won't be fun like it used to be." She arranged her packages beside her on the floor. A woman brought coffee and a plate of cookies to our table.

"I would just like to skip Christmas this year," said my new friend after we exchanged names. "But I suppose I should consider my husband. I guess I'm feeling sorry for myself and shouldn't be going on like this in front of a perfect stranger."

"I understand," I said. "It just isn't the same without one's children around. My son won't be home either. Where is your son?"

"He's taken a job in Florida. And yours?"

"He's in Vietnam," I told Mary.

"Oh, I'm sorry. I have no right to complain."

"That's all right," I said. "You see, my son has invited Jesus Christ into his life. My husband has and so have I, and that's really what Christmas is all about."

I could hardly believe I said that. I was actually witnessing! God had taken me up on my offer.

"You are so fortunate," Mary said. "But I wasn't predestined to have such faith."

"Oh, but that's not what Christianity is all about. The good news of Christmas is for everyone. You see, God lets *you* choose. The Bible says in Joshua 24:15, 'Choose for yourselves this day whom you will serve.' "

26

"But how do you do it?"

Excitedly, I reached into my purse and pulled out a little booklet.* "This will tell you how. It gives the basics of how to become a Christian."

My first impulse was to just give it to her and run. But I mustered my courage and said, "Why don't you take this home and, if you want to discuss it further, give me a call."

"But couldn't we read it right now?" she asked.

*Well*, I thought, *if she doesn't care that people at the next table are looking at us, I guess I don't either.* So there we sat in the middle of the bustle of the holiday season, discussing the true meaning of Christmas.

Together we read about God's love for mankind (I used John 3:16, Rom. 3:23, Rom. 6:23) and how sin has separated man from God. We read that Jesus Christ was God's only remedy for sin (Rom. 5:8, John 14:16). We read Revelation 3:20, where the Lord Jesus says, "Here I am! I stand at the door and knock. If anyone hears my voice and opens the door, I will come in and eat [fellowship] with him, and he with me."

I took a sip of my coffee, which had now gotten cold, then said, "Christianity is a relationship with Jesus Christ. It's something like a marriage relationship. We love and respect our partner. We speak to and delight in one another. If one does all the talking and the other just listens, it's a lopsided relationship. It has to be a two-way street."

*The booklet I use is *The Four Spiritual Laws* distributed by Campus Crusade for Christ. I like it because it forces people to face their spiritual condition. The booklet begins, "God loves you and has a wonderful plan for your life." I qualify that by saying that plan is salvation from sin. If I didn't qualify it, an eighty- or ninety-year old might say, "But my life is almost over."

"I pray all the time, but I never read the Bible," Mary confided.

I nodded. "That's what I mean. The Bible is God's Word. He speaks to us through it. That's really the best part of the relationship. Through his Word, he tells us how to live and what pleases and displeases him. The wonderful part is that he created us to have fellowship with him."

I gave Mary the booklet and, being too timid to press the issue, I asked, "Would you call me and let me know if you decide to invite Christ into your life?"

"I'll be in touch," she promised.

When Mary and I parted, I was so happy to have had my first experience of being available to the Lord in that manner.

I finished my shopping and was on my way out of the mall when I felt a tap at my elbow. It was my new friend, Mary, who was saying, "I just wanted you to know that I have invited Jesus Christ into my life."

I could scarcely believe my ears. I thanked God for the privilege of leading Mary to Christ.

Some time later, she confessed to me that before she accepted the Lord Jesus into her heart she had had periods of depression; but since then, the depression has never returned. Her whole personality has changed. She has become a happy and radiant Christian.

### Reflection

That morning, for the first time, I had prayed, "Lord, I want to be available to you. Please lead me to anyone you want me to speak to." I am continually overwhelmed at God's love and mercy. Here was Mary, a needy soul. She had attended church all her life but

28

never had been given the Bread of Life. There was I, desiring to share a bit of my spiritual food. So God brought us together.

From that time on, I have practiced being available to God. I started noticing people and became more friendly in general. God guides me to people he wants me to witness to. He is faithful to his promises.

He has told us through Moses in Deuteronomy 31:6, ". . . Be strong and courageous. Do not be afraid or terrified because of them [your enemies], for the LORD your God goes with you; he will never leave you nor forsake you."

God has said in Isaiah 55:11, "So is my word that goes out from my mouth: It will not return to me empty, but will accomplish what I desire and achieve the purpose for which I sent it."

Almighty God has promised these things. He will never go back on one thing he has promised. It is our responsibility to walk in the good of every word of God.

# 2

## What To Say When . . .

### *A Stranger Says, "Aren't You a Sight!"*

**Another Mary**

One cold winter morning it was necessary for me to go to the bank. Four inches of snow lay on the ground, so driving was hazardous. I was glad to get safely inside the bank and welcomed the warmth it offered.

While standing in line, minding my own business, a woman I had never seen before came up to me, looked me up and down, and said, "Aren't you a sight—scruffy flat shoes and fur coat!"

I was stunned. I felt like saying, "You don't look so great yourself." Instead, I laughed.

"I suppose I do look rather ridiculous," I admitted. "You see, I've recently had my feet operated on and they're still swollen. I would have liked to have worn my dressy boots, but these garden shoes are the only ones I can get on my feet." I lifted one foot out in front of me and showed her my shoes.

"Because it's so cold out," I continued, "I wore my fur coat. I thought I could get away with looking like this. But I never get away with anything! You know, God never lets me get away with a thing either."

It was her turn to be stunned. "What does God have to do with this?" she asked.

"I teach a women's Bible class and have discovered that God is interested in every aspect of our life."

Then she looked at me very seriously and said, "I don't know anything about the Bible. I probably should. Can anyone attend your class?"

"We'd love to have you come." I gave her my address and telephone number and told her the time we meet. I was looking forward to seeing her again. But she didn't come to the study group. I was disappointed.

A year later, I received a telephone call. A woman's voice said, "My name is Mary. You probably don't remember me, but I met you in the bank."

Before she could say another word, I said, "Oh, yes, I do!"

We both laughed. And then, with a voice that was close to tears, she said, "I have some serious problems. I thought about you this morning and wondered if you would be willing to help me."

We set a time and I waited for her but once more she didn't come. And I never heard from this Mary again. I felt badly and wondered what had happened to her.

Thoughts began to plague me. Did I say something I shouldn't have? Or was there something else I should have said but didn't? She had not given me her full name or address, so I had no way of getting in touch with her. Then the Spirit of God reminded me that I was just a

31

tool. None of us can guarantee the results. Our job is to be faithful to the Lord, to be available, and to take the opportunities he gives us. I think of this woman often and pray for her. I don't even know if she is still alive. I wonder if it was fear that kept her away. Only God has the answer.

### Reflection

Fear does strange things to people. Since it paralyzes and is never productive, fear is the greatest hindrance to witnessing I know. I have been speaking on the subject of witnessing for several years now and, time after time, people come up to me and say, "I want to witness, but I'm afraid."

When I ask them what they're afraid of, the answer is always the same: "I'm afraid I won't be able to answer their questions."

I discovered a few years ago that though a person has a Ph.D. in many subjects and may be an "intellectual," if she doesn't know the Scriptures, she is ignorant of God's truth and needs to get acquainted with it.

My pastor once asked me if I would disciple a woman who had just accepted Christ. I do that sort of thing often, and I enjoy working with people on a one-to-one basis.

I met Doris the following Sunday morning in an office at church. She was in her early fifties. Nothing about her seemed impressive. She was rather short and was dressed very plainly.

I introduced myself and told her how happy I was that she had accepted Christ as her Savior. She seemed excited about having a Bible study. When she told me that she had a King James Version, I suggested that she might want to get a modern translation, that it might be a little easier to understand.

"I prefer the King James," Doris said.

"That's fine," I answered. "I just thought it would be easier for you."

"But, you see, languages are my field," she told me.

"What do you mean?"

"Oh, I teach Russian at Wayne State University."

Talking with Doris further, I discovered she had three Ph.D.s. All of a sudden she became a threat to me. I became fearful and tense. My words didn't flow quite as easily as before.

I went to my pastor and told him about it: "I think you've got the wrong person discipling Doris. I'm not an intellectual. Did you know she has three Ph.D.s?"

"Yes, I know that. I purposely didn't tell you," he said with a twinkle in his eyes. "But, you see, she doesn't know the Scriptures, and you *do*. That's why I sent her to you. You have something she needs."

As I worked with Doris, my fears subsided. She truly was a needy person, and God was using me to help her grow as a brand-new Christian. I needed that lesson. You see, God has not given us "a spirit of timidity, but a spirit of power, of love and of self-discipline" (2 Tim. 1:7). The fear does not come from God but from the enemy who wants to defeat us.

# 3

## What To Say When . . .

### *Someone Asks About "Earning" the Right to Witness*

### Distorted Ideas

Other misconceptions about witnessing can hinder people. Let me tell you about a couple of distorted ideas I've run into.

I was sitting in a church service. The speaker's voice boomed, and his finger seemed to point straight at me as he asked, "How many souls have you won to Christ this year?"

I trembled, not with fear but with indignation. I thought, *Where in Scripture does it say that we are responsible to win anyone to Christ?* We are commanded to witness (Matt. 28:9). Only God gives the increase.

After the service, I waited to talk to the speaker. I introduced myself and said politely, "I didn't know that

God held us responsible for winning a certain number of souls to Christ. I thought our responsibility was to witness."

His answer floored me. "If you witnessed to forty people each day, surely someone would accept Christ."

All I could think of was the hard-sell approach—collar-grabbing. For me to talk to forty people a day, I'd have to go to a mall and grab everyone in sight. The prospect left me depressed. I had seen enough of that kind of forceful witnessing, and I knew it usually didn't work.

Then I read a book and saw a film that said we had to "earn" the right to witness, and that left me puzzled, especially when one of the women who saw the film asked me, "How do I know when I've earned the right to witness?" But I think I found the answer.

I knew we could not earn the right to witness, any more than we could earn our salvation. Actually, since when do we have to earn the right to share good news? We are commanded to be witnesses. It's an order from the Lord. We are to go into all the world and teach all nations (Matt. 28:19–20); we're to witness for him in Jerusalem, and "to the ends of the earth" (Acts 1:8). Proverbs 11:30 tells us that the fruit of the righteous is a tree of life, and he who wins souls is wise. We are told to be wise as serpents and innocent as doves (Matt. 10:16). Common sense tells us not to rush people. We need to be sensitive. I could not find either collar-grabbing or earning-the-right as concepts in Scripture, yet I had a burning desire to be an effective witness.

The Holy Spirit assured me that he had already shown me what to do. I knew I needed to fill my head and heart with the Word. I knew I needed to remain transparent before him, confessing my sins as he brought

35

them before me. I knew I must lean on him as my source of power in resisting the devil, just as I knew I needed to keep being available to his leading. This means keeping my eyes and ears open as opportunities presented themselves to me to speak for my Lord. My problem was that I was in too much of a hurry and was insensitive to other people's needs. I realized that I had to get out of my comfort zone.

For example, I used to hate grocery shopping. I would rush in and out of the store, hurrying to get home to my sewing or to my arts and crafts. Grocery shopping had become a necessary evil. In fact, everything I ever did used to revolve around myself and my interests. Now I take time to look around at others standing with me in the grocery line. I find people fascinating, and many of them have hurts and needs. Often, merely a smile and a word of encouragement can make a difference.

I have gradually learned to become always available to others. I talk to the people waiting with me. Look for cracks in the conversational door as witnessing opportunities to be taken. People often put their real thoughts in the little "asides" they make as they talk. They slip off the topic and insert a statement or opinion that shows how they really feel. I listen for these and pick up on them. I don't want to let my not being sensitive to these clues be the factor that denies anyone the answer to life.

I have found that I don't have to look for lost souls or force the Good News upon them. I don't have to wait "four months" for the harvest (John 4:35). I have opened my eyes and looked on the fields and, I tell you, they are ripe!

## Reflection

The day after I made my new commitment to Christ to be available as his witness, things began to happen. It has been an adventure with God that takes priority in my life. Paul knows that if I don't get home in time to have supper ready at a certain hour, it's because the Lord has opened somebody's heart and given me the opportunity to minister. His support has released me from the tyranny of time. In our lives, the Lord and his interests come first. Both of us truly love the gift that God has given me.

I will be telling you about my experiences with Sue and Bill, with Chuck, with Barbara, with Al, and with many others to whom I have witnessed. As I do, keep in mind Jesus' words in John 4:36–38:

> Even now the reaper draws his wages, even now he harvests the crop for eternal life, so that the sower and the reaper may be glad together. Thus the saying, 'One sows and another reaps' is true. I sent you to reap what you have not worked for. Others have done the hard work, and you have reaped the benefit of their labor.

Many of those I have led to Christ have been previously witnessed to by someone else. This reflects what is said in Isaiah 28:10: "For it is: Do and do, do and do, rule on rule, rule on rule; a little here, a little there."

As we share Christ, we have an opportunity to be part of God's plan and to do his work. All of us who are in the family of God are automatically on his staff. How great it is to work for the Lord!

# 4

## What To Say When . . .

### A Young Woman Says, "My Life Is Such a Mess. I Want to End It All"

**Katy**

Eighth-grade Sunday-school girls generally bubble over with either constant excitement or mischief. My friend Ola and I team-taught a class one year and had a wonderful time individually. But sometimes it did take both of us—especially to pray.

Katy was different from the rest of the girls. It was hard to get a word out of her. She came to class every Sunday, but she just sat there, kind of sad-looking. Ola and I prayed for her and went out of our way to be kind and pay special attention to her.

"We've decided," I announced one day in class, "that those of you who have perfect attendance for the next three months will be treated to dinner at Howard Johnson's. Our husbands will pay the bill, and you can have anything you want to eat."

They were delighted with the prospect.

And then I reminded them, "A little less talking and a little better behavior in class will be greatly appreciated, too, I might add." I said this with a twinkle in my eye so they would know I wasn't upset with them.

They smiled back. They had gotten the point and did make a slight effort afterwards.

Ola and I loved the girls and had already decided that their behavior was normal for their age. Perhaps not amazingly, their attendance and decorum records for the next three months were very good.

"Ola and I are very pleased with your attendance," I told them. "It looks like our husbands are going to have to work overtime to pay for this crowd's dinners."

The girls loved that.

"What I need to know is whether your parents will be able to bring you to the church. Does anyone need to be picked up?"

Katy raised her hand. "I have no one who will be able to drive me to the church." She hesitated. "I would like to come, though."

"No problem," I said. "It's practically on my way."

I was glad I picked her up. It gave me a chance to meet her mother. I had wondered what she would be like. Actually, she was just like Katy, quiet and withdrawn.

During the outing, as the girls in the class began to tell jokes and relate funny stories, we all laughed. They were so funny that even Katy had a faint smile on her face. She seemed to be enjoying herself. After dinner and a few more hilarious jokes and lots of giggles, it was time to leave.

"We've had loads of fun and good food," I said to them all. "And I believe our friendship and love for each other has grown. We probably won't be meeting like this any more, since you'll all be graduating into another department." I loved it when they groaned, since I felt it meant they had accepted Ola and me. We needed that because we wondered many times if we had ever gotten through to them that we loved them.

As Katy and I drove home together, she opened up and became surprisingly talkative. "I had such a good time tonight. I want to thank you for picking me up," she told me. Then it was as if a torrent had broken loose. "I wish my mother was like you. In fact, I wish you were my mother."

"Why, Katy, you surprise me. You have a mother who loves you, I'm sure."

"She never talks to me unless she's scolding. I never do anything right. She's been like that ever since my brother committed suicide."

"Oh, Katy. I didn't know that. I'm so sorry. Your mother must really be hurting. She needs you to love her."

"She doesn't want my love," Katy said. "She wants me to go to live with my aunt for a while. I guess I'll go. I think my aunt likes me."

My heart ached for this young girl.

"Katy, have you ever invited Jesus Christ into your heart?"

"I'm not sure. When the minister preached and asked people to come forward, I was too scared to go up in front. But I wanted to."

"Would you like to be sure you're a Christian?" I asked her.

"Yes, I would."

I knew that she had heard the plan of salvation many times, but it was the application to her life that I questioned. So, in a very simple way, I explained to Katy about God's great love in sending his Son to die for her. If she would receive him as her Savior and Lord, she would then be a child of God.

Timidly, she whispered, "Would you help me pray?"

I prayed the sinner's prayer a sentence at a time, and she repeated it after me.

When we finished, I said, "Katy, I sense you have lots of needs. But now you can talk them all over with your heavenly Father. He really cares for you. When you go to live with your aunt, take your Bible with you and read a portion of it every day. It will be a great help and comfort to you."

Soon after, Katy left town to live with that aunt in another state, and it was several years before I saw her again. When she appeared at church one morning, I hardly recognized her. Katy was extremely thin and hard-looking and no longer the shy, quiet, little girl I remembered.

"How about coming home with us for dinner?" I asked, wanting to get some meat on her bones and spend some time with her.

"I won't be able to today," she said. "May I come during the week?"

"Anytime," I answered. And Katy did begin coming any time she felt like it.

I was really shocked at the change in her. Where she had once been quiet and shy, now there was an air of aggressiveness about her. I also noticed that she became very demanding of my time. "I'm jealous of your children," she told me.

My children had gone out of their way to be kind to her. They invited her to our game time, but she refused, saying, "Thanks, but I'd rather go for a walk with your mother."

I went along with her at first, until it was apparent that she was trying to shock me with her lifestyle. She told me things like "I've taken up smoking. Of course, I can quit any time I want to," and "I'm thinking of getting a job as a nightclub dancer." Once she said, "There are a lot of men who want me. I just can't keep them away."

"Katy, you've committed your life to Jesus Christ," I said. "You know what you're telling me is wrong. It hurts me to hear this; but more than that, you're grieving the Holy Spirit."

"I know. But when I quit, he'll forgive me."

"You're playing with fire. I wouldn't want to be in your shoes."

Katy seemed defiant and unresponsive to my words. She seemed determined to go her own way. My husband and I prayed for her, but we finally decided we couldn't allow her to disrupt our family time any more.

One night, Katy called and said, "I hate my life. I've decided to commit suicide."

Ordinarily, I would have panicked; but I was very calm when I asked, "Why do you want to kill yourself?"

"My life is such a mess. I just want to end it all."

"How do you wish to do it?" I asked in a steady voice.

"I'm going to eat a whole bottle of aspirin."

"Katy, that won't kill you. It'll only give you a terrible, terrible stomachache. Why don't you come over and we'll talk." I don't know what made me say that. It scares me every time I think about it. But it worked, and I was grateful to God.

When she arrived at the house, I put my arms around her and said, "I love you, Katy. I'm glad you changed your mind. Whatever made you even think of such a foolish thing?"

"I'm pregnant. I have no money. I hate the father. I won't marry him, and I want to keep my baby."

"You can't keep your baby if you take your life. Actually, you'd be taking two lives, yours and the baby's."

"I'm so confused and mixed up. I don't know what to do," she admitted.

Then we prayed together and I assured Katy of our love and support. Later we found a Christian counselor through our church. He helped her deal with her situation.

Katy insisted on keeping little Debra after she was born, and she truly loved that baby. But she had so many struggles. Her health was failing. She never ate properly (her main diet was Cokes and hamburgers), and she wasn't able to get rid of her smoking habit, though she had tried.

About nine o'clock one evening, she called. "I went to the Bible bookstore tonight. I bought a picture of Jesus talking to the little children. I'm going to hang it over Debra's bed. Mrs. Pickard, I want you to know that when I saw that picture, I realized that I don't want my baby to have the kind of life I've had. I want to raise her to know about Jesus, and I want to be a good mother. I want to help her all I can to be an obedient Christian. I've been so rebellious, and I'm so very sorry. I don't know how the Lord can ever forgive me, but I got on my knees tonight and asked him to take me back and help me live the rest of my days for him. Now I'm asking you to forgive me. I know I've been a big disappointment to you and taken so much of your time—and your family's time."

"Oh, Katy," I said. "Of course we forgive you. That's what Christianity is all about."

"Thank you," she said. "I have such peace and love in my heart. Thanks for your patience."

I shared Katy's words with Paul, and together we gave thanks to God for the good news.

I was awakened the next morning by the ring of the telephone. My friend's voice sounded excited but strained when she asked, "Have you heard about the fire?"

"No, what fire?"

"Katy and the baby. They found her in the middle of the living room floor, holding the baby. She had tried to cover Debra with her own body."

The newscasters said the fire had started in the bedroom. They figured Katy was in the kitchen when she smelled the smoke and ran for the baby. But she couldn't get to safety.

It is such a bittersweet story—but I'm glad Katy called me that night. Perhaps it was God's mercy that took her home.

### Reflection

Katy's mother had tried to hide her own hurts from her daughter, but shutting her out only made her feel unloved, which was reflected in Katy's behavior, first in her withdrawal from her peers and then later in her defiant bitterness. Both were clues to her desperate need, and it took a long time for Katy to discover that God would never shut her out. He was always there with his love and forgiveness, always ready to take her back. She finally felt that peace in her heart.

Our family schedule was interrupted and inconvenienced by Katy many times. There were times when we felt our efforts were useless. "Why bother?" we would ask ourselves. Then the Spirit of God would remind us that we are not our own. We are bought with a price. We are not to satisfy the flesh but must be available to God to help heal the hurt of those who have been caught in the trap and snare of the evil one. (For further study, read Romans 12.)

# 5

## What To Say When . . .

### Your Neighbors Think You Spend Your Time Passing Judgment on Them

#### Marie

"Has Nellie converted you yet?" my next-door neighbor laughingly asked Marie, who lived a few doors down the block and told me about the incident later.

"Not yet, but who knows!" she answered lightheartedly.

Even though Marie was not a Christian, she was a friend and would not allow anyone to laugh or scoff at us.

It was well noised-about among our neighbors that we were Bible-believing Christians. My children were small then and were pretty good little advertisers. Things went pretty well until my older daughter, Karen, then eight years old, informed Mrs. Brown that she was destroying God's temple by smoking and would never go to heaven if she continued.

That upset some of the neighbors. They became uncomfortable with us and apparently felt we spent our time sitting in the house passing judgment on them. We learned that Marie told them that Karen was just a child, adding, "Nellie and Paul don't talk about neighbors like that. Don't take it so seriously."

Marie came to us after this incident, and we had an opportunity to tell her our biblical beliefs: "Yes, we did tell Karen the reason we don't smoke is that it is harmful to our bodies. Our body is the temple of God, and we must take care not to harm it. And we didn't tell her that Mrs. Brown would go to hell if she smoked!"

Not able to have children of her own, Marie was especially fond of our little Greta and came down to the house quite often. Many times in the summer, she would invite us to have lemonade and ice cream in her yard. Greta loved visiting Marie and begged to see her every day.

One day Marie confided in me as we were sipping coffee together, "You and I are so different in our backgrounds and lifestyles. I drink and smoke all day long and yet I hate it. My husband cheats on me and I'm miserable. You, on the other hand, don't have any bad habits and you have a husband who adores you. You seem to be happy all the time. You're so lucky."

"Oh, not lucky, Marie," I said. "I'd say I'm blessed. It's not that I'm so great. I just have a great God." I touched her hand. "He can turn your life around the way he did mine, if you allow him to take charge. You can have peace in spite of all your problems."

"Do you think that's possible? Don't you think it's too late for me?"

"It's never too late," I told her. "God would be so pleased if you'd turn your life over to him. You see, he gave his only Son to die on the cross for your sin—and mine. He did that because he loves us so much. The Bible says that in John 3:16."

"I think I've heard that verse before—when I was a kid," Marie said.

"Did you know that Jesus came to seek you? And to save you? And that he wants you to be his child?"

"I guess I've heard that before, too. I really want to belong to him."

Then we prayed together, and Marie thanked Jesus Christ for dying especially for her. She asked him to be her Savior and Lord.

Her husband later told his friends that his wife had gotten religion, which he thought was funny. He flaunted his women before her, leaving evidence of his behavior around as though to mock her. He was in the National Guard and, one time, while he was away at camp, my husband suggested that the children and I take Marie on a vacation. Paul would join us at the end of the week. We went to lovely Lake Michigan and had a great time. We swam, hiked, and had cookouts; but the best time was our Bible study and Scripture memory sessions.

"I love it," Marie said. "I can't believe I'm actually quoting Scripture." We all prayed together. The children, all three of them, loved having her around and were on their good behavior all week.

Some time later, we both moved away in opposite directions. We saw each other only occasionally. Marie's husband died and she remarried a year later. One day she called and asked, "Do you have some Bible-study books my husband and I can work on together? Neither one of us is well, and I think this would be helpful." I was most happy to send them to her.

I was speaking at a Christian Women's Club luncheon some time later when I spotted Marie in the audience. It was such a pleasant surprise.

As she was leaving, we talked and she handed me a note to read later. It said, "My husband and I probably won't have much time left. We are both very ill. We are leaving for Oklahoma to spend our last days with my family. I want you to know that today I rededicated my life to Jesus Christ. Thanks for speaking to me again."

### Reflection

It's very possible that you, a faithful Christian witness, will suffer from teasing and tongue-wagging. Some Christians, as well as non-believers, seem to be uneasy around those who take the Lord seriously. King David was very conscious of this and prayed about it in Psalm 31:19–20:

How great is your goodness,
  which you have stored up for those who fear you,
which you bestow in the sight of men
  on those who take refuge in you.
In the shelter of your presence you hide them
  from the intrigues of men;
in your dwelling you keep them safe
  from accusing tongues.

We can't stop people from talking and from trying to throw our witness into a bad light. But we can do what we can to correct false impressions, as we carry on faithfully, trusting the Lord to use us as he wants. Let people talk and criticize! We are sheltered in the Lord's dwelling, where we can rest in him and not be offended or harmed by idle gossip.

Being loved ourselves, we can love others. Marie came to Christ because we loved her and she loved us. Through our love, she found the love of the Lord.

# 6

## What To Say When . . .

### *She Says, "Having Just Had a Brush With Death, My Thinking About Life Has Changed"*

**Fran**

One of the most exciting aspects about leading someone to the Lord is that no two experiences are ever the same. Every person is unique, and every situation involves a different set of circumstances. We must learn to be alert and sensitive to the individual needs of the people we meet. It is usually these very needs that provide an opportunity for us to witness for the Lord.

Take, for instance, my meeting with Fran, which happened one afternoon at poolside. But let me start from the beginning. . . . My husband and I had purchased a condominium in Florida, and we were involved, as were many other new owners, in decorating our vacation apartment. No matter how busy we were, though, we always managed to take time for a daily swim or a walk on the beach.

One afternoon, while I was taking my break at the pool, I was introduced to Fran, an attractive, outgoing woman who was experiencing the same frustrations I was in dealing with broken delivery promises from furniture companies. While we were comparing notes, Fran mentioned that she had been in bed for several weeks. Naturally, I picked up on her comment and asked, "Have you been ill?"

"While I was swimming in the ocean," she said, "I was stung by a Portuguese Man of War. That's a horrible, poisonous sea animal with long tentacles; and the pain was so intense I had to stay in bed for weeks. This is my first week out, and I'm so happy to be up and around."

We talked about her unfortunate accident and got better acquainted that afternoon, but it wasn't until several months later that I actually had an opportunity to share my faith with Fran.

I met her on the beach one morning. Remembering how ill she had been after the Man of War encounter, I asked, "How are you feeling?"

To my surprise, she said, "Right now, I'm recovering from a cancer operation; but I'm really not concerned because, you see, I have faith."

Well, this was something to explore.

"Faith in what? Would you tell me about it?"

At this point, she became flustered and stammered, "Well—uh—ah—I really don't know exactly what to say, because I guess I don't know God. I was hoping you could help me. Someone at the apartments told me you had your head together about God, so I made the trip down here hoping to find you so you could help me."

She stopped for a moment and looked out at the surf. Then she said, "You see, having just had a brush with death, my thinking about life has changed." There was a quiver in her voice. "Knowing more about God is very important to me now."

I was both flabbergasted and pleased. I was flabbergasted because here was Fran asking me to share my knowledge about God, when normally I am the one searching for an appropriate opening. And I was pleased because I evidently had a convincing testimony and had sown the seed with someone at the apartments. God was using that seed in this experience. I silently thanked him for giving me what I call another "divine appointment."

I never know exactly what direction I will take with a person until the situation presents itself. Then I rely on the Holy Spirit to give me the wisdom to say and do the right thing. In Fran's case, the key was that she wanted to know about God, so I promptly began to respond to her need, knowing she was anxious to be helped.

"Do you have a Bible?" I asked.

"No," she admitted.

"Well, it's very important, when you want to know God, to read and study the Bible. One of the books in the Bible, Romans, says in the seventeenth verse of the tenth chapter that 'faith comes by hearing the message,' and this message is the Word of God. That means that if we want to have faith, we must listen to what God has to say in his Word, the Bible."

Fran was so eager to get started that we immediately left the beach, got dressed, and went together to purchase a Bible at a local bookstore. I suggested that she start reading in the Book of John, and then we could discuss the next day what she had read.

I thought she would read just a few chapters, but she told me the next day, "I stayed up reading until two o'clock this morning, and I read the entire Book of John." I felt she had a real desire to know the truth and that she wanted to make up for lost time.

Before we discussed her reading, Fran shared some things about herself. She was a very busy, financially secure woman who was involved in three different businesses. As she talked, I had an overwhelming desire to help her find the abundant life that Christ came to give.

"Do you remember reading John 3:3?" I asked. "Jesus says, 'I tell you the truth, no one can see the kingdom of God unless he is born again.' "

"I think I remember that verse," said Fran.

"Well, just as a baby is born into a human family, so must a person be born into the family of God. As a baby needs milk and food to grow physically, the Christian needs the Word of God in order to grow and mature spiritually. When a Christian neglects reading God's Word day after day, he begins to experience malnutrition just the same as a human being does when meal after meal is skipped."

Fran listened closely, but I sensed she needed more time to read and talk about God's Word, so I didn't press her for a decision.

The next day I was sitting on my balcony when I saw her on the beach below, reading her Bible. We had spent so much time together that I thought she might like to be left alone for a while. But she looked up and saw me and yelled, "Come on down!"

I quickly put on my bathing suit and went down to the beach.

"Before I saw you on the balcony," Fran said, "I asked

God to please send you down. I really want to know more about the Bible. There's so much I don't know."

I sat beside her and we began with John 3:16. "Read it out loud," I said.

She read Jesus' words: "For God so loved the world that he gave his one and only Son, that whoever believes in him shall not perish but have eternal life."

When Fran finished, I explained: "You and I deserve to die for our own sins. But Christ willingly bore all of our sins on the cross for us. He actually took our place and died the death that we deserve. If we believe that and tell God the Father that we want to stand in the good of the death of Christ for us, he will grant our request and forgive our sins. He will give us everlasting life." I continued, "Look here at John 3:17, the next verse: 'For God did not send his Son into the world to condemn the world, but to save the world through him.' We make the choice either to receive Christ as our Savior or to reject him."

Fran took in everything I said, as if each word was a precious gem. She said she had a lot to think about. "Why don't you and I go out to dinner tonight?" she suggested.

I sensed she was very close to making a decision for Christ. "I'd love to," I said.

We went to a restaurant overlooking the ocean. The sun was beginning to set, and the view was breathtaking. *Only God could paint such a scene as this*, I thought, knowing also that only God could perform a miracle in Fran's life that night.

Though the waitress approached our table several times to see if we were ready to order, each time Fran would tell her we were not. She was filled with questions about God and Jesus and was so eager to know the answers that eating was hardly on her mind.

We finally ordered our dinner, but it took us almost two hours to complete it because of Fran's insatiable desire to know and understand God's Word. Our meal got cold as we got more and more involved, but neither of us cared, since we were both fulfilling our needs— mine to witness to Fran and Fran's to know God.

Returning to my apartment, I suggested we read that little "Four Laws" booklet I often use. It presents the plan of salvation in a simple, concise way. When we finished, I said, "Fran, would you like to accept Christ as your Savior?"

"Oh, yes!" she replied, as if there was not a doubt in her mind.

We bowed our heads and prayed, and Fran asked Christ to be Lord and Savior of her life. It was such an emotional moment for both of us that we cried tears of joy.

Before Fran left, I explained to her that she was now like a diamond in the rough. God would be chipping away to make her the kind of person he wanted her to be.

I received a letter from her a few weeks later. In it she told me she had gone to her jeweler and asked him to make her a ring with two stones—one a green, bumpy unfinished diamond and the other a white sparkling one. "I know that right now I'm like the green, bumpy one," she wrote. "But as God chips away at my life, I'll become more and more like the beautiful white diamond."

### Reflection

I could never have dealt with Fran in this manner if I had unconfessed sin in my life. As mentioned earlier, I'm learning to keep short accounts with my Lord.

Now, you might be frightened by the realization that Fran asked a lot of questions at dinner that I didn't include in my story. I'll expand on that conversation now, but I want to say first that you may not have all the answers to questions people ask you. When that happens to me, I simply tell them, "I can't answer that now, but let me have time and get back to you." This keeps me from giving a hasty answer I haven't thought through, and it also creates an opportunity to resume the conversation later.

Fran did say, "As a teenager, I attended the Jehovah's Witness Kingdom Hall. I went with my aunt. I didn't feel comfortable in that church. They don't believe you should salute the flag, and they don't believe in blood transfusions, no matter how desperately a person may need them. Do you know about the Jehovah's Witnesses?"

"The last time I talked to them," I said, "I told them I would allow them to come into my house if they would allow me equal time to share my faith. They said they would; but, when it was my turn to speak, they kept interrupting so much I finally had to ask them to leave. You see, they don't believe that Jesus is God in the flesh. When I showed them the first chapter of John, which says that Jesus is the Word of God that became flesh, and that he, Jesus, is God, they denied it and said that Jesus is *a* god. But, Fran, that means they believe there are many gods—and that's idolatry."

(I might mention here that reading about cults in the light of Scripture helps us to "always be prepared to give an answer" to those who ask about our reason for hope [1 Peter 3:15]).

"But how can you be sure the Bible is the Word of God and that it's true?" she asked.

"There are many proofs," I said. "One is the changed

lives it produces. Second Corinthians 5:17 and 18 says that if anyone is in Christ, he is a new creation. That's what happened to me. Actually, that's why some of the people in the condo say I have my head together about God. Another reason is that many predictions made in the Old Testament are fulfilled in the New. For example, prophecies about how Christ would die and that he would rise from the dead were recorded hundreds of years before they happened.

"It's interesting to read about those who have read the Bible with an open mind and have been convinced of the truth. Even some who have set out to prove that Jesus Christ is a fraud have fallen on their knees begging forgiveness after reading what the Bible has to say. One of these men is Lew Wallace, who was a famous general. After his conversion, he wrote the novel *Ben Hur.* Another is C. S. Lewis, a professor at Oxford. One of his post-conversion books is *Mere Christianity.* Both men were convinced that the Scriptures are authentic."

Fran was an eager listener. I had found a heart that was ripe for the Savior.

I saw Fran in Florida recently. She is a growing Christian who is sharing Christ with others. She is delighted that her daughter and son-in-law have also accepted Christ, and all of them attend church together regularly.

Not all of my witnessing experiences, of course, are as easy or as productive as this one with Fran. Sometimes I only get to sow a tiny seed by sharing a thought or giving a word of encouragement or asking a pertinent question. But I rest assured that, however far I am able to go with an individual, God knows and will honor my obedience in being faithful to him.

In a world where people are caught up in all forms of materialistic living and excitement, we must not be deceived by outward appearances. People all around us have needs that ultimately are answered and met only by faith and trust in Jesus Christ. My task, my mission as a Christian, is to uncover those needs and to help people find the One who meets all needs—the Lord Jesus Christ.

# 7

## What To Say When . . .

*A Neighbor Says, "I'd Like to Talk to You—But I'm Just Not Ready Yet"*

**Sally**

**S**he came with some of my neighbors to hear me speak at a Christian Women's Club luncheon. I was both surprised and delighted, as I had previously had only a superficial relationship with Sally. We would say our hellos in passing, remark about the weather or any new bargains we had purchased, but we had never had a serious conversation.

When I had given my message and closed the meeting, I went to the main door, as is the custom for speakers at such luncheons, to greet the people and accept the "comment cards" they had filled out. Three of my neighbors greeted me and gave me their cards—but not Sally. She went out another door.

But, as she walked down the hall past me, our eyes

met. She sheepishly waved, smiled, and called, "I'll see you later."

I thought to myself, *She's afraid to come through the line.* I wondered why.

When I met Sally a few days later, she said, "I want to talk to you sometime—but not now. Maybe next week, maybe next month, or three months from now. I'm just not ready yet."

I noticed as she was talking that she kept walking away from me. She kept her hands up in front of her face like a protective shield and seemed afraid of me for some unknown reason.

"Anytime you're ready, I'll be available," I told her.

Sally has not come to see me—but I'm still available.

### Reflection

It's hard to know what keeps some people from wanting to talk about the one subject most crucial to their eternal destiny. John's Gospel speaks of people who love darkness more than light. Some people are not ready to give up a sin they dearly enjoy. Or perhaps they are afraid. They could be fearful of exposing their inner thoughts to anyone else. Or they could be afraid of me, afraid to confront someone who has a settled faith and intimidated by someone who has victory over sin.

As we saw with the Mary I met at the bank, fear does strange things to people. It paralyzes. Fear kept Sally from hearing God's answer to the abundant life in Christ, and I believe it kept away the Mary who said, "Aren't you a sight!"

As I also mentioned before, I believe fear is also the greatest hindrance for the witnesser. I am sometimes fearful when I first meet someone in need of witnessing, but I have discovered that God is faithful and his words are true. He fills me with his power. The Spirit of God is in me and helps me. The Lord gives me courage and brings to remembrance the things I have studied in his Word.

I have likewise discovered that if I do the possible, God will do the impossible. I cannot make a person believe. Only the Spirit of God can open a heart and show someone the truth.

Another thing I have learned is that the more I witness, the easier it becomes. God was with me the first time I spoke out, and I know he will be with me again and again. You see, when we are doing what he wants us to do, he will always support us.

Linda, a delightful, outgoing young friend of mine, determined she would witness for the Lord at her job. She worked for a nationally known woman psychologist and also for a local radio station. Though the office always buzzed with interesting topics and people talked about everything under the sun, Linda, out of fear, had always kept her faith in Christ to herself.

Finally, Linda's new determination got her right in the middle of sharing her faith. But she panicked. "Oh, Lord, please help me," she prayed.

"And do you know? He did," she told me later, excited by what had happened.

Sharing Christ *is* exciting. After all, it's the answer to life itself. We just can't keep the Good News to ourselves. We can't let fear keep our faith all bottled up. If *I* did, I would explode. Meanwhile I pray that Sally will conquer her fear and tell me she is "ready" to hear the message of hope.

# 8

## What To Say When . . .

### A Stranger Asks If He Can Hug You

**Chuck**

One day I decided to ride my bike down Ocean Boulevard. When I got to the corner, a young man jumped out of the way as if he thought I was going to run into him.

"Don't worry," I assured him. "I saw you coming and was prepared to stop."

"I'm always careful when I see a bicycle coming," he said. "Where I went to school, there were more bicycle accidents than car accidents."

"Where did you go to school?"

"Michigan State."

"My son graduated from Michigan State," I told him.

"Are you here on vacation, or do you live in Florida all year?" he asked.

"We live here part of the year and part of the year in

Michigan. This year, we came early because my father broke his hip. He's almost ninety-nine years old, and we felt he wouldn't have a lot of time left in this life. We want to spend as much time with him as possible."

The young man looked genuinely sympathetic. "I'm sorry about your father."

"Thank you," I said, "but you don't need to feel sorry. You see, my father is looking forward to going home to be with the Lord."

"Did I hear you correctly? Did you say he was looking forward to going home to be with the Lord?" He seemed stunned by my comment.

"Why, yes. He's ready and really excited."

Then the stranger surprised me by saying, "My name is Chuck. Could I hug you?"

I looked at this young man of about twenty-four years of age and said, "If you feel the need of a hug, go right ahead."

He gave me a bear hug. And then he said, "I needed that. I came to Florida feeling rotten. My wife left me three months ago. We had been married for only five months. It really put me in a slump. My uncle asked me to drive him to Florida to help him buy a condominium.

" 'You need a change,' my uncle said. 'The trip will do you good.' But I still feel very depressed. You see, it isn't as though I didn't know my wife before we got married. I dated her for four years before I asked her to be my wife. We both joined a Bible study group. I became a true believer in the Lord Jesus Christ, and I thought my wife had, too. We got married and believed that our newfound faith would make our marriage extra-special. But a few months later, she announced to me that I was too religious and that she was going to go her own way."

"How sad," I said.

"I was absolutely devastated," Chuck admitted. "I've been getting some help from a Dr. Stringer up at State. If it wasn't for that, I don't think I could have survived."

"Are you talking about Dr. Ken Stringer?" I asked.

"Why, yes. You know him?"

"I've known him since he was a little boy. He's one of the finest young men I know. He and I are members of the same church."

Chuck was shaken. "I can't believe this! I simply can't—" Tears came to his eyes. "Our meeting was no accident," he said. "You know, I thought God had forgotten me."

"God never forgets," I said simply. "And I agree that our meeting was no accident. It was one of God's appointments. He arranged for you to meet another Christian, knowing you would be at the beach and that I'd be along. You see, I've told the Lord that I'm always available to him to use any way he wants."

"I suppose you thought it strange for me to ask you for a hug."

"Oh, yes, somewhat. But you looked safe enough. I guess I just followed my instincts."

"Well, I'd just been on the beach talking to a group of people. One of the women asked me if I was married. I told her my wife had just left me, but that I was praying for God's wisdom to work it out. 'How stupid,' she said. 'I suppose you don't believe in abortion either.' "

I interrupted him: "That was a strange thing to say. It sounds as though she realized that God wasn't in favor of abortion."

"Well, that kind of talk didn't make me feel any better," Chuck admitted. "I walked on down the beach and met a young man wearing earrings. He tried to solicit me. I couldn't believe it. Two days in Florida and this is what I run into! Then when you said that your father was looking forward to being with the Lord, I went from the slough of despond to sheer joy. I finally found someone on my wavelength. I just had to hug you."

I invited Chuck to have dinner with us and to meet my father. They became instant friends. Chuck felt free to share his heartache with him, and my dad prayed with him about his needs. The next time I saw Chuck, he said, "To see a man ninety-nine years old so full of the joy of the Lord—and at his age and in his condition to have a concern for others—is something I won't ever forget. I want to be a growing Christian and end up knowing God like your dad does."

### Reflection

Chuck, a new Christian, had some wonderful things to learn about God's care for him. Remember that God promises, "Never will I leave you; never will I forsake you" (Heb. 13:5b).

Psalm 139:2–3 says, "You know when I sit and when I rise; you perceive my thoughts from afar. You discern my going out and my lying down; you are familiar with all my ways."

Here again, as we tell God we are available to him to meet the needs of people, he will use us to minister to those who hurt.

(By way of note, I had a husband at home. I would never have invited Chuck to my home had I been living alone—nor should any woman, even when the aim is witnessing!)

66

# 9

## What To Say When . . .

### She Says, "I Know All That. It's Not Going to Help Me!"

**Nicole**

"I'm very concerned about Nicole, a friend of mine," Pam, a young lady I was discipling, said at one of our sessions. "Would you be willing to go with me to see her? I have already told her about our Bible studies and she would like to talk to you."

When I first met Nicole, she was the picture of despair. She wasted no time telling me about her problems: "Peter and I had been having an affair for over a year and planned to be married. I couldn't believe it when he said that he wanted to break off our relationship and return to his ex-wife. I begged him not to, but he acted as though we were never close. I've tried calling him, but he won't answer."

I sat in silence, listening to Nicole as she went on:

"My life is such a mess. I don't know what to do. I feel like ending it all. Ever since I was a little girl, I've had nothing but one rejection after another."

"Well, then, I'm glad we got together today," I said, "because I'd like to tell you about the One who came into my life and who has *kept* his promise never to leave or forsake me. That person is Jesus Christ."

Her face seemed to cloud up, but I went on: "I confessed my sin of living my life without him and of going my own independent way. I had never once consulted the Lord about his will for my life. He lovingly forgave all my sins and made me a member of his family. It's the best decision I've ever made in my life. I now have peace and a life worth living. And you can have this life, too."

"I know all that," Nicole snapped. "It's not going to help me!"

I stood up and prepared to leave.

"Oh, please don't go," she pleaded. "I need help with my problem."

I wanted to stay, but it was obvious to me that Nicole wanted Peter back more than she wanted to understand the reason for her predicament. So I said, "I came to tell you that the Lord Jesus Christ is the very best help I can recommend. Without him, there is no real solution to your problem. But you say you 'know all that,' so I really have nothing else to offer."

I walked toward the door.

"Please, may I see you again?" I heard Nicole say.

I thought of my schedule. "You may come to my home next Thursday at eleven o'clock if you would like." I gave her my address and left.

During that week, I prayed that God would prepare her heart and give me the wisdom to know how to help her. But I wasn't sure if she would even come. But she did arrive, and promptly at eleven. I was pleasantly surprised. We sat on my porch and relaxed over a cup of coffee. "Tell me a little about yourself and your family," I prompted.

Once again Nicole seemed eager to talk: "I spent my early years on a farm with my parents, two brothers and a sister. I was only nine when my mother died. My family fell apart. My sister and older brother moved out of the house, and my father, who was an alcoholic, married our housekeeper and left the farm."

"Did you go with your father?" I asked.

"No, my father took off without us. He actually left us on the farm to fend for ourselves. I was eleven and my brother was only nine at the time."

I was amazed. "How did you survive?"

"We lived on the food we found in the cupboard. I remember sitting under a tree, tears streaming down my face and thinking, *I hate grown-ups. I never want to be one.*"

"Someone must have come to your rescue," I suggested.

"Right. One day, my brother and I took a walk down the highway. We met Mrs. Smith, our neighbor, who kindly asked, 'How are things at home, Nicole?'

" 'Not so well,' I told her. 'Bob and I are all alone on the farm. Dad got married and left with our housekeeper.'

"Mrs. Smith invited us to have dinner with her and later called the authorities. She arranged to have us live with her and became our foster mother for three years. A doctor friend of ours was also kind. He counseled me and saw to it that I got a good business education."

"Did things become a little better for you then?" I wondered aloud.

"Yes, life was much better for a while. Then one day I received news that my father had died from overconsumption of alcohol. He was only fifty years old. His death brought on emotions that I had experienced often as a child, feelings of loneliness and dejection."

I nodded my head in sympathy.

"Shortly after my father's death, I met a very successful businessman who made me feel good. He was wealthy and treated me like a queen. We were married and were happy at first. I soon became pregnant and we had a little girl. We enjoyed our baby, but our happiness didn't last long. My husband began to mistrust me. Every time I stepped out of the house, he would accuse me of having an affair. His jealousy became so intense that he would badger me all through the night. I wanted to cover myself up to rid myself of his accusations. We were soon divorced. Once again I felt alone and rejected.

"I lived quietly, adjusting to the change and caring for my daughter. Then Peter came along and showered me with attention. I felt accepted and loved again. He was the answer to all my problems—that is, until he decided to go back to his ex-wife. Loneliness and rejection seem to be the pattern of my life. . . ."

Nicole paused. "You know, when I was with Peter, we had a beautiful relationship. We even went to church every Sunday."

"Do you feel that going to church with Peter made your relationship right?" I asked.

She didn't answer my question, but instead told me, "I'm so afraid that, when I leave here, I'll go home and call Peter. I want to see him so very much." Nicole looked so wistful when she said that.

"Well, you can't have it both ways," I said. "You have to make a choice. It's either God's way or your way."

Quickly she said, "But I do want God's way—and I do need him."

"Would you like to tell him your choice?" I asked her.

She just sat there and looked at me. Then she nodded slowly and began to pray: "Lord Jesus, I confess I've gone my own way, leaving you out of my life. I need you and receive you as my Savior. Thank you for forgiving my sins and for opening the gates and letting me walk through."

That was a new beginning for Nicole, though the next few weeks were rough ones for her. She called me several times a week, crying on the phone. She was having a hard time putting her life back together again. The temptations of her old life were still strong, but God gave her strength. We met for Bible studies once a week for a while.

Her little girl has also received the Lord Jesus as her Savior, and the two of them read the Scriptures and pray together. Nicole has joined a Bible-believing church and is now an active participant in its fellowship. She recently accepted a very good job and is already considered to be one of the top sales reps in her firm.

Nicole is a very attractive person, and she tells me she is often approached by men. "Do you know what I tell them?" she said one day. "I tell them I'm not interested, that I've been there. I now have a new quality of life in Jesus Christ."

### Reflection

Nicole was miserable when I first knew her and hardly needed me to point a finger at her. To her, life was not worth living without Peter. She wanted a fairy-tale ending, but sin had robbed her of that possibility. I gave her the only solution I knew—a right relationship with Jesus Christ. But she wasn't ready for that at first.

I had nothing more to say to Nicole at that point. She needed time to reflect on what I had said and time for the Holy Spirit to do his perfect work in her heart. Though I knew she was hurting, I couldn't comfort her in her unrepentant sinful condition.

I was glad when Nicole wanted to see me again. That meant she had not shut the door entirely and that I had another opportunity to bring to her attention that her lifestyle was a complete offense to God and that she would have to make a choice—her way or God's. Nicole learned that her way led only to despair, but God's way brought her peace. It was a hard lesson, but she learned it.

We had many good times together after that. We played tennis and she came to our home for dinner many times. We had Bible studies together. She learned quickly. Now, Nicole is no longer the picture of despair. She's a beautiful, radiant Christian.

As 1 Corinthians 10:13 says, "No temptation has seized you except what is common to man. And God is faithful; he will not let you be tempted beyond what you can bear. But when you are tempted, he will also provide a way out so that you can stand up under it."

Let us point out to hurting people that guaranteed way of escape!

# 10

## What To Say When . . .

### She Says, "It Really Doesn't Matter What You Believe, as Long as You're Sincere"

**Harriet and Shirley**

Sometimes I can scarcely believe the situations in which God places me. Take, for example, what happened one day when I was purchasing supplies to make a decoupage purse. That's exactly how I met Shirley . . . but I'm getting ahead of my story.

One Sunday at church, I had seen my friend Sally's latest decoupage purse and remarked with a slight tinge of envy, "Sally, your purse is beautiful! I would love to have one just like it." Sally is very gifted in arts and crafts. She makes enamel flowers, tole paintings, and many other beautiful craft items. Her decoupage purses are simply exquisite. Many of her friends and I had often prodded her to teach us.

A couple of days after that Sunday conversation, Sally called. "Nellie, I would be willing to teach an arts and crafts class if you think we could use it as an outreach to win some neighbors to Christ." I agreed at once that it was a great idea, so we began planning for our class.

Our church has a Christian day school, and we were able to obtain the use of the art room for our project. Sally would teach decoupage and I would give devotions. We spread the word and the class started. About twenty-five women came.

I, too, wanted to make a purse as part of the class, so I went to a nearby arts and crafts store to get my supplies. Only one other customer was in the store besides myself, which I later found was quite unusual. The other customer was a rather elderly woman. As I was looking through the supplies, I heard the owner of the store, whose name was Shirley, say to her, "Harriet, your work is superb! It is absolutely beautiful!"

I turned to see Harriet smile. In fact, she beamed as she said, "This is quite a day for me. I'm going to receive an award today from my church for all the good work I've done."

My ears perked up. This was interesting. Since I was a brand-new customer and had never been in the store before, I didn't want to intrude on the conversation. But then Harriet added, "You know, it really doesn't matter what you believe, as long as you're sincere." To my surprise, she turned to me and asked, "Don't you agree with me?"

I reached over and touched her arm gently and said, "I'm sorry. I can't agree with you. You see, that isn't scriptural. The Bible tells us that salvation is not by works, but by grace, which means it is unearned favor. It's a gift from God. We receive it by faith."

"Now, what is that all about?" Harriet asked.

"I have a little booklet [*Four Laws*] in my purse that explains God's requirements for a right relationship with him. Would you like to take it home and read it?"

Shirley, the owner, had been listening and suggested, "Why don't you read it to us?" And I did.

I read of God's great love in sending his Son to die on the cross for our sins and of the purpose in Christ's coming—to give us abundant life. I read how our sins have separated us from God and that only Jesus Christ could bridge the gap between man and Holy God—not our works, not a good life, nor even being "religious." I read how each individual had to receive Christ and that when we receive Christ by inviting him to come into our lives to cleanse us and to forgive us and to take control and guide us, we then experience the new birth.

I looked at the women and asked if they would like to receive Jesus Christ as their Savior.

Shirley said, "I can't believe that you're standing there and I'm standing here. You're answering a need I've had in my life for months. Two years ago, I was asked to demonstrate decoupage at a Christian Women's Club. When I was finished, I told the hostess I needed to get back to the store and asked if she minded if I left.

"She said, 'Yes, I do mind. I think you ought to stay and hear the message.' What could I do? So I stayed and heard the same thing you've told me today. I didn't take it too seriously because I didn't feel the need for God in my life. Then, three months ago, my father had a stroke. Now he can't walk and he can't talk. He was such a handsome man and an active golfer. He was a dentist and now he can't do a thing except sit in his wheelchair and be waited on. It breaks my heart. On top of that, my husband lost his executive position in a large advertising firm. For some time I have wanted to reach God, but I couldn't remember what the speaker had said. And now you've come here and told me the way."

Shirley bowed her head and asked Christ to come into her life, to forgive her sin and make her his child.

When I turned to Harriet and asked her if she would like to receive Christ, she looked at me and said, "I'm not going to give up eighty years of good works for this." Then she left, having made her choice.

But my contact with Shirley did not end that day. Often, when I witness to someone, I am given the opportunity to meet and reach other people in that person's life. So it was with Shirley; this was just the beginning.

For a year I met with her for Bible study on Tuesday mornings before her shop opened. It wasn't always easy. The phone would ring or a customer would knock on the window, hoping to get in early. The interruptions seemed endless, but it was thrilling to watch Shirley grow as a young Christian.

Shirley's business was very good, but the emotional strain of her father's illness and her concern about her husband's job finally made her decide to sell the shop. An added burden was her increasing worry about her mother's spiritual condition. Her mother, Ella Foster, had told Shirley she thought Christians were pushy. She wasn't interested in listening to her daughter tell her one thing about her newfound faith in Christ. Then one day Shirley asked me if I would be willing to visit her folks.

"I'll do it," I said, "but it might take a year before I'll be able to talk to your mother about Christ. Remember, you told me about her saying Christians are pushy."

And it did take exactly a year before Mrs. Foster came

to Christ. I visited her about once every two weeks. I would bring her flowers from the garden or something I had baked. I would sit and listen as she poured out her heart. She and her husband had shared such a good life together. They had had so many friends, but now only one of his colleagues ever came to visit. They found life very hard.

One day Mrs. Foster said, "I've been doing most of the talking. Please tell me something about yourself and your family."

I told her some of my delightful stories about my children—the nice things mothers tuck away in their hearts. Then I told her that my younger daughter, Greta, had come down with an illness called lupus when she was a senior in high school.

"The doctor told me it was treatable but not curable," I said. "I couldn't believe it. She had been such a healthy child and this had come on so suddenly. I fell flat on my face, but it was only momentarily. You see, I knew that God made every cell in Greta's body and had counted every hair on her head. He loves her more than I possibly could. Together, my husband and I committed this situation to the Lord and we have had peace.

"One day, as I visited Greta in the hospital, we talked about her condition and I told her she had a choice to make. She could either become bitter and say, 'Why should this happen to me?' or she could use this experience as an opportunity to grow. And you know what she said? She said, 'That's what I want to do, Mom. I want to grow. You see, I believe in God because you told me about him. But now I've had my own experience, and I know he's with me.' "

I could see that Mrs. Foster was moved by my story, so I went on: "Through the kindness and tutoring of her teachers, Greta was able to finish high school at home, where she stayed in bed for three months. She had been accepted by Gordon College before being hospitalized, but now we thought she wouldn't be able to attend college—especially Gordon, which was eight hundred miles away. Greta was very excited about going and would talk constantly about her plans, but there was no way of explaining to her that she just wasn't well enough.

"We talked with the doctor about this. He said, 'If she were my daughter, I would let her go. But be prepared to pick her up in about six weeks. At least she can say she went to college.' "

"So Greta attended college—not for six weeks but for four years. There seemed to be an epidemic of flu every year in her dorm, and we were concerned because the doctor had told her to be extremely careful about catching a cold or taking medication without consent. But Greta didn't have the flu or even a cold in her four years at Gordon! We had prayed that God would put a hedge about her, and he did."

Mrs. Foster threw her arms about my neck and wept. Then she said, "I'm so tired and I have so many needs."

"Perhaps I can help you," I offered. "I believe I can, if you will let me." I told her I would see her soon and then left.

As I visited her from time to time, I told her about some of the people I had met and led to Christ. I shared with her exactly how each situation developed and told her what Scripture I had used. She seemed to listen very carefully and was quite interested. Then she told me one day, "I think it's wonderful that you are able to help so many people."

Shirley had given her mother a Bible, and each time

she visited she noticed the Bible was open, so she knew her mother was reading it.

During this time, Dr. Foster became too difficult for his wife to handle and was taken to a nursing home. While on my way to visit him one day, as I approached his room I noticed his door ajar. I heard him calling, "God, oh, God," over and over. I entered the room and found him very distressed. When I asked him if he wanted a nurse, he shook his head, so I stroked his forehead and tried to comfort him the best I knew how.

I explained how he could reach God through Jesus Christ, saying that if he would invite the Lord Jesus into his heart, he would be forgiven of his sins and God would accept him as his very own. Dr. Foster just groaned and seemed more distressed. He tried to talk, but I couldn't understand him.

Next I called Shirley and said, "I think you need to go and tell your father what Jesus Christ has done for you and that you are now in God's family. Tell him you are concerned that he know the Lord as his Savior."

She did just that. Later she told me she had taken his hand and said, "Dad, I've been going to Bible class and we've been studying the Book of John. I've learned so much about Jesus Christ, and I've accepted him as my Savior and confessed him as my Lord. Would you let me read to you some of the things I've learned?" He squeezed her hand as a sign of agreement. He began to relax, his daughter was relieved.

Shirley visited him day by day after that and read to him from John. One day, she said, "Dad would you like to receive Christ as your Savior?"

He took her hand and nodded "Yes." And then he had peace. Shortly after that, he died and went to be with the Lord.

Mrs. Foster, who by then had asked me to call her Ella, asked if it would be possible to have a little memorial service just for the immediate family and a doctor friend who had been faithful in visiting her husband during his illness. She also wanted me to be there, as well as our mutual friend, Sally Roost, and asked me if I thought the pastor of my church would say a few words. I felt that now was the time to ask Ella about her relationship to the Lord.

"Tell me, Ella," I said, "we've talked a lot about how some of the people I've met along the way have come to know Christ. What about you?"

"Oh," she said to my delight, "when you first told me how, I accepted Christ as my Savior."

I have known Ella for some time now. She has a hunger for the Word and truly loves the Lord. Every time I was asked to speak someplace, Shirley and her mother would be there, constantly learning and still excited about the Word of God.

All of this happened because I visited an arts and crafts store as one of my scheduled errands for that day and took the time to respond to a human need. But the story does not end even here.

My husband and I spent Christmas in Florida that year. Before we left, Shirley asked us to stop in to see her widowed aunt in West Palm Beach if we were in that vicinity. Shirley loved her aunt and was very eager for her to meet us. "She's attended church all her life, but I know she's not born again."

We visited Shirley's Aunt Ann on Christmas Day. She was all alone and, despite the fact that she was almost blind and had a difficult time moving about, she had an outgoing personality and welcomed us warmly into her home. We introduced ourselves as Shirley's friends and told her how we had become friends, including how Shirley had come to know Christ. I explained that her niece was now in the family of God, that she had been born again.

"Would you explain to me about being born again?" Aunt Ann asked. "I've listened to Billy Graham talk about it many times, but somehow I didn't think it was for me. You see, I attended my church for forty years, and they never told me about it. The minister visits me from time to time, but he never mentions it. Please tell me more."

I told Ann about Christ's purpose in coming to earth. I told her that God's love is so great that he gave his Son to pay the penalty for our sins. When we accept the fact that he died for us because of love, and when we receive him as our Savior, we are born again.

"Would you like to receive Christ as your Savior?" I asked.

"Are you sure it's for me?"

I read Revelation 3:20 to her, then said, "Jesus invites you. It's up to you to accept his invitation."

"If it's for me, I want it," Ann replied. She prayed with me and invited the Lord Jesus Christ into her life. She was born again on Christmas Day.

Shirley was so very happy to receive a letter from her aunt, telling about her salvation experience. Six months later, Aunt Ann died and went to be with the Lord.

How marvelous that four people in that family became saints of God out of my one small visit to an art store!

### Reflection

Witnessing and sharing the love of the Lord Jesus is not something mystical or scary, something reserved for a select few who feel called to the ministry. Neither is it homework that you do for church. Rather, witnessing can become a completely natural part of your everyday life. It can be as common and routine as the daily functions of eating and sleeping. It can be as life sustaining and invigorating to our spiritual well-being as those functions are to our physical lives. As we are earnest, ready, and willing to practice witnessing, God will instruct us and guide the process.

Over the years, I have learned that witnessing is something I can develop and improve just like my cooking, sewing, and typing. It's a matter of practice—combined with a right relationship with Christ and a genuine interest in the people I meet during my normal routine of daily living.

On occasion, I am bold and will speak right up to any "Harriet" who asks me a direct question about eternal things. On other occasions, I don't rush things. For example, I offered to let Harriet take the booklet home and read it. It was Shirley's idea that I read it right there in the shop. And, with Ella Foster, I took time. I never pressed her. When she said she was tired and had so many needs, I said simply, "I believe I can help you if you'll let me." I said I would see her soon and left.

Now, realize, no one can do something exactly the way someone else does it and retain any kind of spontaneity or relaxation. We must trust the Holy Spirit to lead us and not try to create or follow a recipe of how people must witness. I believed I was to touch Ella lightly and to come back again and again. As I did this, she learned to trust me. Had I been as bold with Ella as I was with Harriet and Ann, I'm sure I would have offended her.

Each of us must trust the Lord to help us do the right

thing. And, once we've done it, we must rest and not
fret. Faith is perhaps as important a part of witnessing
for the witnesser as it is for the one to whom we have
witnessed.

Remember that!

# 11

## What To Say When . . .

### A Shopper Admires a Nightshirt That Says, "When I'm Sleeping, I'm a Saint"

**Debbie**

The shopper standing next to me, looking through the lingerie rack, pulled out a nightshirt and started to laugh. "How would you like to wear this?"

My ears pricked up at the woman's beautiful British accent, and I turned to see what she was looking at. On the front of the shirt was written, "When I'm sleeping, I'm a saint."

We both laughed, and I felt the freedom to speak after we introduced ourselves. "It's interesting how many people think that if a person's sleeping or doing nothing or merely behaving himself, this automatically makes him a saint. That's not what the Bible says a saint is."

"I know," Debbie said. "A person is made a saint after he or she dies, by a group of bishops or religious higher-ups." Since her voice implied a question mark, she didn't seem to be quite sure about that.

"Well, in the New Testament, the apostle Paul wrote letters to people he called saints," I commented. "Sometimes he called them 'believers,' but those people were alive and serving God. Today, when we become members of God's family, we, too, become saints. We may not always act very saintly, but that's what God calls us."

"Well, if you don't act saintly, why does God call you a saint?"

"He does demand perfection," I agreed, "and none of us is perfect. But Jesus Christ is. We come to God through Christ. Christ serves as the bridge between the sinner and the God who demands perfection. In John 14:6 Jesus says, "No one comes to the Father but by me."

"I have some very nice friends who are Christian Scientists. You make me think of them. Are you one?" Debbie asked.

"Oh, no," I said gently. "I'm not. You see, a Christian Scientist doesn't believe that Jesus is God. But the Scriptures say that Jesus is God in the flesh."

"Hmmm. That's interesting," she said. "Tell me where you go to church."

I told her and added, "My husband and I are presenting a series of films on 'The Holiness of God.' It's a six-week study. My husband first reviews the previous week's lesson, and I lead the discussion after the film has been shown."

"May I come to your class?" she asked.

"We'd love to have you come." I gave her directions. Before she left, she said, "I believe God meant for us to meet today."

I prayed for Debbie during that week. I didn't know whether she would actually come to church, but on Sunday morning, as I was helping my husband arrange the chairs, I felt a tap on my shoulder and heard a familiar voice saying, "Can you tell me where I can find Nellie Pickard?"

It was Debbie—and I was delighted to see her there.

The film shown that day was "Holiness and Justice," part of the series produced by Dr. R. C. Sproul. First, the story of Nadab and Abihu was read from Leviticus 10, where God destroys Aaron's sons for failing to follow the letter of the law in the matter of the Holy of Holies, that part of the tabernacle where only the High Priest could go once a year. A second story, from 2 Samuel 6, told of Uzzah, who was struck dead when he reached out and touched the Ark of the Covenant, which God had forbidden anyone but the priests to touch.

These were not easy passages to deal with, though they did help us understand the sovereignty of God and that we—as his subjects—cannot tell God how to run his kingdom. He gives the orders. The lesson also showed what rebellious creatures we are.

I wondered how my friend would receive the message.

When we finished class discussion and ended the meeting with prayer, Debbie called across the room, "Nellie, may I talk to you before you leave?"

"I'll be there in a minute," I said. "Just let me put my papers away."

When I reached her, she said, "I have some questions I want to ask you. When we talked at the store, you said that God demands perfection. Am I right?"

"Yes, I said that. The Bible says none of us can reach God's standards. We just can't make it on our own."

"You also said that I could come to him through Jesus Christ. Is that correct?"

"That's correct," I said. "Now would you like to hear the rest of the story?"

"Very much," she said.

We found a couple of chairs and sat down to discuss God's wonderful plan of salvation. We talked about sin and how it separates us from God, and I explained how we don't have to stay in that condition of being a sinner. God has provided a remedy, the Lord Jesus Christ, the Perfect One. We read from 1 Corinthians 15, which tells us that Christ died for our sins, was buried, and that he was raised on the third day and was seen by his disciples and later by more than five-hundred people.

"You know, Debbie," I said, "Jesus died for the sins of the whole world. That includes you. He died for you as an individual. That means that you as an individual need to receive him as your Savior and Lord. It says in John 1:12, 'Yet to all who received him, to those who believed in his name, he gave the right to become children of God.' Another thing the Bible says is that our salvation is by grace. We don't work for it. We can't work for it. It's a gift. That's what it says in Ephesians 2:8 and 9. If we could work for it, we would have a tendency to brag about what we had done.

"You told me in the store, Debbie, that you felt God meant for us to meet. Perhaps this is the reason, so that you could find out how to be in the family of God."

"Probably," she said seriously.

"Would you like to pray and ask the Lord Jesus to come into your heart and forgive your sins?"

"I would like to do that." And she did.

Later, Debbie told me that she had planned to go to a religious retreat that weekend but told her husband that she felt it was very important for her to go to see a woman she had met at the store. "I felt such an urge to see you, and now I know why," she added.

We have met together several times since for Bible study and fellowship. I am delighted with her answers, especially since not too long ago she didn't know the Bible contained both a New and Old Testament. Now Debbie is learning to find the references quite well. Having gone to church most of her life, she had previously done some teaching, though she had never searched the Scriptures for herself.

God must have a sense of humor. After all, he brought us together over a silly nightshirt!

### Reflection

Who would ever think a conversation over a store display could be an opener for witnessing? That, however, is part of the witnesser's mind-set. Any little casual circumstance can be a crack in the door, an opportunity we do not want to miss. We may not know where such a conversation will lead, but God does—and he uses our availability.

A few years ago, I probably would have laughed about the nightshirt along with the woman and let it go at that. Since I now have a better knowledge of the Word, I realize that, even though the statement on the nightshirt was funny, it wasn't true.

Here was my opening—my chocolate-covered cookie— and I went for it!

# 12

## What To Say When . . .

### The Tennis Pro Says, "I Attend Church Only at Christmas and Easter"

**Al**

"The new pro at the tennis club is a real go-getter," Marge told me. "He's trying to sign everybody up for tournaments."

"Sounds like fun," I said. "Don't know how long I'll last, but the competition ought to be stimulating. Let's sign up."

Four of us from church played doubles together every week, and Al, the pro, was pleased when we came to sign up for his program.

"You'd better mark the schedule on your calendars," he said. "The tournament will last for six weeks and will be held on Wednesdays and Sundays."

"Well, I guess that lets us out," I said. "Most of our Sundays are taken up at church." The other gals nodded their heads. We all agreed.

"Don't you go to church, Al?" I asked.

"Not on a regular basis," he said. "I attend church only at Christmas and Easter."

"Oh, you're really a loser," I said, chiding him a bit.

"Why do you say that?"

"Well, anyone who only goes to church on those two days has to be the loser."

Al suddenly became serious. "It wasn't always that way," he said. "I used to go to church all the time. When I was in college, someone from Campus Crusade led me to Christ."

He told us that he grew as a Christian for a while and was happy in the Lord; but, as time went on and the pressures of life set in, he became discouraged: "I got more and more involved in Sunday sports, and the things of the Lord just sort of became dim. I had a hard time remembering how good the Lord had been to me."

"It's when we forget God that we become losers," I pointed out.

"But things weren't going right for me," he explained. "I had problems in my marriage. I became bitter and angry with my wife. I guess I was angry with God, too."

"When we become angry with God, we cut ourselves off from the very best help possible," I said. "Did God cause your problem?"

"Of course not," he said. "But I expected him to bail me out."

The other women had backed away when they saw that the conversation was going to get personal. Al had not noticed, and he continued talking. "I know I'm wrong. I've been wallowing in self-pity and suppose I ought to do something about it. I really have been thinking about going back to church, but I'm new in this area and don't know where to go."

"Why don't you come to our church next Sunday and then have dinner with my husband and me afterwards?" I suggested.

Al did come to church and was greatly moved by the pastor's message. The Spirit of God did a work of grace in his heart, and he confessed his sin of backsliding. He joined our home Bible studies and once again began to grow in the Lord and to fellowship with God's people. The joy of the Lord returned to his life. We could all see it.

Later, Al moved back to New Hampshire, but he kept in contact with us for a while. In the last letter we received, he wrote, "I have recently been baptized and am thinking of going to the mission field to help keep books for the missionaries."

I can no longer call Al a loser. He's a sure winner!

### Reflection

Athletes don't ever like to be called losers, but Al *was* a loser. I just had to be frank in helping him confront himself and see himself as God sees him. Most of us are reluctant to do this as we witness. We feel so vulnerable to counterattack that we sometimes don't speak up at all. Actually, *we* are the ones on solid ground, reaching out to help those in the mire, and we should act on that basis.

I was glad my friends moved back out of the way. It's important, when someone under conviction is addressing one person, that the others either keep quiet and pray, or that they leave and pray somewhere else. Matters of the heart are personal, and we need to allow those talking to have all the privacy we can give them.

Notice that I invited Al to my home, though I had

never met him before. But here was an ailing and disappointed believer who needed help and counsel. I do open my home when I feel it is appropriate. In this way I can back up my words of love and encouragement with actions, often with Paul's assistance. I can prepare a nice meal, and my husband and I can show our new friends they are really special.

I include this story because a true witness is faithful to speak at all times. Sometimes the listener may be a believer, and that's fine. The important thing is to let God work through you when and where and how he wishes.

# 13

## What To Say When . . .

### *A Jewish Man Asks If You Resent His People Because They Did Not Accept Christ as Messiah*

**Joe**

"May I ask you a question?" I quietly asked a young man as he finished paying his bill at the checkout counter at K-Mart.

"Why, yes," he answered politely.

"Because of the little black cap you are wearing, I presume you are Jewish. Am I correct?" I asked.

"Yes, I am."

"Would you be an Orthodox Jew?"

"That I am."

"I'd much rather talk to an Orthodox Jew than a Reformed Jew," I said, "because I find that the Orthodox Jew knows so much more about the Scriptures."

At that, he turned and looked directly into my eyes. "Are you a Christian?" he asked.

"Yes, I am."

"Do you resent the Jews because they did not accept Christ as Messiah?"

"Oh, no," I answered. "We can't *make* others believe. Only the Spirit of God can reveal the truth to your heart."

"It's sure a great relief to know that not all Christians resent Jews," he said.

"As a matter of fact, we Christians owe a great debt to the Jews."

"How is that?" he asked.

"Well, the oracles of God were originally given to the Jewish people, and almost all the New Testament writers were Jews," I said.

"That's true. And Jesus was Jewish, right? Do you believe that the Jews are God's chosen people?"

"I most certainly do. Do you know why they were chosen?"

"No, I don't have the slightest idea," the young man admitted.

"They were chosen so they might tell the Gentiles what God is all about. But they failed. Now we Christians have to tell the Jews what God is all about."

I was surprised when he said, "I don't know how the Jews could tell the Gentiles what God is all about when they don't even know themselves. Have you ever heard the story of Cain and Abel?"

"I know it well."

"Remember that Cain's sacrifice didn't please God?"

"Yes, I remember," I told him.

"Well, God told Cain that he could still make it right."

"That's true," I prompted.

"Now we can go on the rest of our lives making things right with God."

I decided not to comment on that statement.

"When did they start calling people Christians, anyway?" he asked.

"It was at Antioch. Haven't you ever read the New Testament?"

"Oh, no. We're not supposed to read it. I shouldn't even be talking to you about these things."

"Why don't you read the New Testament—not to believe, but to find out what it's all about? For instance, we were just talking about Cain and Abel. Why didn't Cain's sacrifice please God?" I asked.

"Well, it was supposed to be a blood sacrifice."

"Exactly. Cain was angry when his sacrifice wasn't accepted. God asked him why his face was so downcast. If you do what is right will you not be accepted? (Gen. 4:6, 7). Cain was not willing to come God's way, he wanted to please God his own way.

"Throughout the Old Testament, God required a blood sacrifice to make atonement for sin. It had to be a perfect spotless animal—a lamb or a ram. The interesting thing is that in your Bible, the Old Testament, in the fifty-third chapter of Isaiah, it speaks about Jesus Christ being that lamb that took away the sin of the world. Have you ever read Isaiah 53?"

"We only read the five books of Moses," he said.

"Well then you are not getting the complete picture of the Old Testament.

"Lots of lessons can be learned by reading Joshua, Judges, Ruth, and the Psalms. They are wonderful books. And then there are the prophets. Do you know that their prophecy had to be 100 percent correct or God had them stoned for being false prophets? They could foretell only what God revealed to them. Only the truth could be predicted."

"Maybe I should read them," he said.

"It's exciting to read the prophets. Why, if the Jeanne Dixons were doing their predictions in Old Testament times, they would have been put to death because they're not always correct in their predictions."

My husband had finished paying our bill and joined us. The young man introduced himself as "Joe," and we told him our names.

"This man has the impression that Christians resent Jews because they didn't accept Christ as Messiah," I said.

"Oh, no," Paul said. "True Christians love all God's people. Many of them put their own lives in danger for Jews persecuted during World War Two."

"Mmmm, that's good to know," Joe said. "I'm glad you reminded me." He seemed to want to leave.

"Nice talking to you," Paul and I both said, and we were on our way.


### Reflection

I sought out that conversation because the young Jewish man was wearing his little cap—a *yarmulke*—in public. He was making a statement that everyone could read—that he was Jewish. I believe that gave me the liberty to take the initiative and talk to him about what he believed. It's important to do this. Jews need to talk to individual Christians. They have so many misconceptions about what we think of them and what we believe. Only direct, yet gentle, conversations can clear up these ideas.

We want to encourage these sincere people to read God's Word for themselves. Only very rarely will Jewish people respond to a one-on-one witness and receive the

Savior then-and-there. But, as they read the New Testament, God the Holy Spirit can illumine their minds and hearts and draw them to himself.

It was my responsibility to give this young man clear and direct answers to his questions. Years ago, one of my Sunday-school teachers had told our class it was important for us to know that it was at Antioch that people were first called Christians—"belonging to Christ." I couldn't figure out then why that was so important. This day I knew why.

We who belong to Christ must be ever alert to the opportunity for enlightening others about the gift of salvation that is offered to all people who understand and believe "what God is all about." Those "others" include Jewish people who have not yet accepted Jesus Christ as their Messiah.

It is also important that we keep our ears open when we are instructed by any teacher of God's Word. We must be a learning people so that, as 1 Peter 3:15 says, we may give an answer to every man who asks us to give "the reason for the hope" that is in us.

# 14

## What To Say When . . .

### Someone Seems Happy in a Cultist Church

**Maude**

Maude seemed happy in the Christian Science Church. The members had been kind to her when she had a real hurt in her life, and she had many friends among them. Maude was a most gracious octogenarian. While visiting her sister-in-law, Joyce, in Florida, she attended services at our church with her. It was conference time, with two services four times a week, and going to all the meetings as well as the Saturday-night dinner and concert was no easy feat for an elderly woman.

This woman did not look her age, eighty-six. She dressed well, carried herself beautifully, and was "a lady" in every sense of the word.

When I met Maude, I said, "Are you enjoying your vacation in Florida?"

"Why, yes, I am. I'm especially enjoying these meetings and the speakers. It is all very good."

Joyce couldn't understand what Maude meant by that. The next time I saw her she said, "I'm really stumped. Maude is having the time of her life, and yet I know she isn't saved. Would you be willing to have lunch with Maude, her daughter Janis, and me, of course? Maybe you'll get a chance to talk to her about the Lord."

"I'd love to," I said. "And if the Holy Spirit provides an opportunity for a discussion, I'll certainly try to be sensitive to the situation. But we do need to be careful about pushing her into something she's not ready to accept. Let's all pray about it and see what comes."

I was rather surprised when another friend from church, Ruth, showed up at the restaurant. She had held Bible classes in the church and was well versed in the Scriptures. The thought came to me, *Four gung-ho Christians—and Maude. Poor soul, she doesn't have a chance!* But I prayed, "Dear Lord, please take charge."

The food was delicious, and we chatted for a while about the beautiful weather, the ocean, tennis, and how great it was to be in Florida. It didn't take long before our conversation got around to spiritual matters.

"You certainly have had some inspiring speakers at your church this week," Maude volunteered.

"Did you agree with their messages?" Ruth asked.

"Yes, pretty much."

"What do you think of the virgin birth?"

"I believe Jesus was born of a virgin," Maude said.

"Do you believe the Bible is the Word of God?" I asked her.

"Yes, I do."

No matter what was asked, Maude had a good answer, until I asked her if she believed that Jesus was God in the flesh.

"No, that I don't believe," she admitted.

"What about sin? Do you believe that Jesus died for your sins?"

"I believe Jesus died for the sin of the world. He already did that, so he didn't have to die for *my* sins."

On the one hand I felt sorry for Maude. One against four. On the other hand, I admired her. She did not seem one bit ruffled by our questions. She handled herself with dignity and composure.

When we finished our meal, Maude insisted on paying for all of us. "I've had such a good time and I want this to be my treat," she told us.

I walked Maude to her car. On the way, I said, "I have a workbook that is called 'The Uniqueness of Jesus.' There are questions to be answered, and the answers must be looked up in the Bible. You can learn a lot about who Jesus Christ is by studying these lessons. Would you be willing to spend some time on this book?"

She smiled and said, "Because I like you, I will do it." I was delighted. We drove to my apartment so I could get the book. "Maude, when you have completed these lessons, would you mind sending them to me and letting me know your conclusions?" I requested.

When she left, I thought, *How gracious she is.* Then I prayed that the Spirit of God would open her eyes and heart to receive the truth of the Scriptures as she began her studies.

Soon after that, Maude went back to her home in Tennessee. I learned that her daughter Janis called her from time to time and would always ask, "How are you doing on your Bible lessons?"

Once, Maude had answered, "I tell you, Janis, I'm not going to do those lessons, because I do not believe that Jesus is God."

"But you promised Nellie!"

"I don't care," said Maude.

"But does a Christian Scientist go back on her word?"

"Oh, all right, I'll do them," she agreed.

Janis herself was growing as a Christian and was very concerned that her mother would turn to Christ, too. After all, at eighty-six, Maude might not have many years left. So Joyce and Janis and I covenanted to pray for her.

When I arrived back in Michigan from Florida, I waded through the mail and to my delight noticed an envelope with Maude's return address on it. I quickly opened it and, sure enough, the workbook was completed. She had answered all the questions. I carefully read each one and it was incredible. The answers were perfect.

Paul looked at what Maude had done, commenting, "Do you think she just copied the answers from the Bible? Or do you think she really believes what she's written?"

"I sure hope she does. I'll call her." I couldn't wait. I picked up the phone and dialed.

"Maude? I got your lesson book. You did a beautiful job. The answers are perfect. Tell me now, what conclusions have you come to? Do you believe that Jesus is God?"

"Oh, Nellie, absolutely," she said. "Do you know that after doing my lesson, I went to my Christian Science study book, and it said that Jesus is a son of God. I said to myself that this wasn't enough. So I went back to the Bible and it said Jesus *is* God. If the Bible says it, it has to be true."

When I got off the phone, I told my husband what she had said. "There's only one thing I failed to mention,"

I said. "I should have asked her about sin. I wonder if she now believes that Jesus Christ died for *her* sin."

I started to write Maude a letter, then threw it in the wastepaper basket. I picked up the phone and called her instead. "Maude, I don't want to leave any stones unturned." I asked her that important question.

"Oh, yes," she said, "I've asked Jesus Christ to be *my* Savior, and I also know that he is the only way to God."

### Reflection

The booklet I used with Maude was "The Uniqueness of Jesus." It is the introduction to *Ten Basic Steps Toward Christian Maturity*, published by Campus Crusade for Christ, San Bernardino, California. See how valuable it was in reaching an intelligent person who was steeped in the teachings of another doctrine? Sometimes, when our words seem to fail completely, we can refer a person to a workbook like this that will require her to study the Bible. The Holy Spirit works through the Word. As I have said, it's incredible! New birth is a spiritual matter, not something we work up or produce. Though a workbook will often help us find where an unbeliever is hung up, we must remember that coming to Christ is not an intellectual decision.

This story about Maude shows that "faith comes from hearing the message, and the message is heard through the word of Christ" (Rom. 10:17). We must remember also that "the Word of God is living and active. Sharper than any double-edged sword, it penetrates even to dividing soul and spirit, joints and marrow; it judges the thoughts and attitudes of the heart" (Heb. 4:12). (Study John 1 for the heart of "the message.")

Maude has completed five workbooks on the different aspects of the Christian life. She's amazing!

# 15

## What To Say When . . .

### *A Young Man Says, "I'm Really Depressed About My Life"*

**Jim**

**M**y fellow patient was a pitiful sight. His head was completely swathed in bandages, except for two peepholes for his eyes and a slit for his mouth. His room was next to mine at Straith Memorial Hospital, where I was recuperating from a foot operation. I knew his operation couldn't have been life-threatening since that hospital does only elective surgery.

One afternoon as I hobbled down the hall I saw him coming toward me. We stopped and talked. We both laughed as we noticed the many bandaged heads and feet, most of them victims of an almost frivolous desire to enhance appearance.

"If I didn't know better, I would say that this is a place for the maimed and infirm," I said laughingly.

Then, looking at his bandages, I asked, "What happened to you? Were you in an accident?"

"No, this was no accident," he told me. "This was on purpose. I had a face-lift, a nose job, and two hair flips for my receding hairline."

I thought it was quite unusual that a man would want a face-lift, especially one whose voice and gait suggested that he was quite young. We chatted casually over the next few days, and I sensed a loneliness and hurt about this young man, who had told me only his first name, Jim.

When the bandage was removed from his nose, I said, "It looks like they've given you a good-looking nose. I don't know what it looked like before, but it looks very nice now."

"It was very large before," Jim said. "I also had very deep lines in my face. I looked pretty bad. I want to improve my looks for my wife, but I don't think she really cares about me. In fact, I don't know what's going to happen to my marriage."

The day he was to leave the hospital, Jim came to my room. Even though most of his face was still bandaged, I could tell by his body language that he was still dejected.

"What's the matter?" I asked. By that time I felt he knew I was his friend.

"My wife just called me, and I feel awful. She's angry with me because I didn't pick a hospital closer to our home. She's a busy person and is annoyed that she has to drive five miles farther to pick me up."

I couldn't believe a wife would say that to her husband, though I had noticed that he had not had any visitors.

Jim continued, "I'm really depressed about my life.

But I do know one thing, that I couldn't make it without God."

"I'm glad to hear you say that," I said. "Have you been born again, and are you a member of God's family?"

"I don't know anything about that. I only know that I need God in my life."

My roommate and the nurses were walking in and out and making it difficult to talk, so I suggested, "We obviously can't talk here. Why don't you take this booklet to your room? It explains God's requirements for becoming a member of his family."

He held out his hand for it and turned to leave.

"When you're finished," I said, "please come back and let me know if it makes sense to you. By the way, there's a prayer at the end of the booklet. I suggest that you read it, think about it, and see if that meets your need."

Jim left and about an hour later peeked into my room and asked, "Could we talk?"

"Sure. Come on in."

He had tears in his eyes as he said, "Thanks for caring. That message is just what I needed. I prayed the prayer and received Jesus as my Savior."

Though Jim apologized for crying, his tears kept coming. Finally he went into the washroom at the end of my room and sobbed. When he had composed himself, he came back and thanked me again for caring. Then he was gone.

His name was Jim. That's really all I know about him, but I hope my witnessing helped him sort out his life.

### Reflection

Helping a stranger who is hurting is rarely easy, but the love of God should constrain us to do it. If we stop to ask ourselves, "What am I getting into?" we are like the priest and the Levite who saw a man lying half-dead after he had been stripped and beaten by robbers. They passed by on the other side of the road, not raising a finger to help.

I am glad the Samaritan stopped and helped that man. We—following the pattern of our Lord Jesus—are to be Samaritans, too. We need to be inconvenienced at times, to be reminded that we are not here to serve ourselves but to serve others. In doing that, we serve God.

Since Jim was a married man and I am a married woman, it would not have been good judgment on my part to directly comfort him when he was weeping or to try to follow him up after we both left the hospital. However, I have prayed that God would send someone into his life to help him grow in the knowledge and love of his newfound Savior. Sometimes this is all we can do.

I wouldn't know Jim now if I met him on the street, but I'm comforted by the thought that he who knows the number of the hairs on our head certainly knows Jim and will provide for him.

# 16

## What To Say When . . .

### *She Says, "I Think I'm Going Crazy!"*

**Laurie**

I had just started to wash my hair and was thinking about the young people's meeting held in our home the night before, when the phone rang. A distraught voice at the other end pleaded, "I'm Laurie. I was at your home last night, and I need to talk to you. I'm desperate. I didn't sleep all night. I think I'm going crazy! Please, may I come over right now?"

"Give me an hour," I said as the water trickled down my neck. "I'm in the middle of washing my hair. Come over about eleven."

I hung up the phone and thought, *I don't even know this woman.* We had had quite a number of young adults at the house, and I couldn't remember her. I was even more perplexed by the fact that she said she was going crazy. I wondered whether her distress was mental or spiritual. Before I finished my hair, I made a quick call to my husband. "Paul, you need to pray for Laurie," I said as I explained the brief details and then felt reassured by his support.

When Laurie arrived at my door, I saw a very pretty young woman whom I vaguely remembered from the night before. Although she had said she was desperate, she now appeared to be in control.

"Hi, won't you come in?" I smiled and led her out to my favorite sunny porch. It was apparent that she was nervous and uncomfortable, so I quickly tried to put her at ease. "Would you like a cup of coffee?" I wanted to reassure her with my voice and my smile.

"Yes, please." She followed me into the kitchen.

"Do you work or go to school?"

"I'm going to school, and I'm in between jobs right now," Laurie replied.

Sensing her difficulty in telling me the real reason for coming over, I said, "Why don't we pray and ask for God's blessing and help as we talk together." And then I prayed: "Heavenly Father, you know all about us, even the deep secrets of our hearts. Thank you for sending Laurie here today; and I pray that, whatever her need, you will give wisdom and direction. May we honor Jesus Christ in whatever decisions are made. We ask in his Name. Amen."

I had barely finished praying when Laurie blurted out, "My big problem is that I don't have what you and some of the people who were here last night have. I feel I'm missing something in my life. Christ seemed to be a part of every aspect of your lives."

She barely stopped for a breath before she went on: "In fact, it was as though Christ was woven into the very fiber of everyone's life here, not just something added. I can't understand, for example, why Craig would spend hours talking to people about Christ on his vacation. That's what really got to me last night. I felt so uncomfortable. Outwardly, I was sitting here and listening, but inwardly, I was screaming. I don't know what you were all talking about!"

"Laurie, I don't think you've ever surrendered your life to Christ," I said. "You've ignored the only one who can give real meaning to life, the Perfect One who can cleanse you from your sin and make you a member of his family."

She looked at me with a sense of awe, then said, "It's as though you see right through me." Lowering her head and voice, she added, "You're so right. I've never surrendered my life to Christ."

"Would you like to do it right now?" Laurie's struggle was reduced to my simple question. The very thing she desperately needed was being offered to her.

She bowed her head and prayed out loud: "Lord, I give you my life and all of my problems. I trust you to work them out, and I want to live for you from now on. I confess that I've been playing at being a Christian most of my life, but now I really want Jesus as my Savior and Lord. I want to live for you."

When she finished praying, she began telling me her life story.

"Believe it or not, I was raised in a Christian home and an evangelical church. At the age of seven, going forward seemed to be the thing to do, so I said I wanted to be saved. I remember that day very clearly in terms of what I wore, but little else. I was too scared and upset to know what I was doing or why. In fact, I didn't say one word the whole time because I was crying so much. When I saw how pleased everyone was with my 'decision,' I decided that if they didn't know I was confused, I certainly wasn't going to tell them.

"As I grew older, I remember thinking how really empty my heart felt. The older I got, the less satisfactory my so-called conversion was for me. Since I knew the talk and walked the walk, I found that as long as I outwardly conformed, nobody bothered me about my heart—except for a small voice inside me. The louder it spoke, the harder I worked. I played the piano, sang, taught Sunday school—you name it. And in time the voice got quieter. Then I didn't hear it any more.

"I hoped to find the security and happiness I longed for in another person, and I married after high school. I worked hard at being a good wife. I tried very hard to find meaning for my existence in the various roles I played and the things I did, but nothing satisfied for very long. I drifted along with no goals or purpose or hope. I certainly had enough to be happy and comfortable by the world's standards, but I was not.

"I guess that to admit I wasn't happy would have been too hard. To say that I was just going through the motions of being a Christian and, in fact, had no vital relationship with Christ would have destroyed the only world in which I knew how to function. I was frustrated and desperate, but I didn't know what to do. If I carefully broached the subject to someone else, I was reminded of all the blessings I had.

"After eight years of an empty marriage, I was divorced. If God was sovereign, why had he allowed the situation to turn out so badly? It was in the months that followed that I resolved to prove just what an ogre God really was. I quit church and all pretense of being a Christian. I had fun—the world's style—but something was still missing, and that nagging voice came back."

"Is that when you began attending our church?" I asked Laurie.

"Yes. I threw myself into church activities all the harder. I copied the actions of my new friends and read my Bible regularly. This time, though, the voice got even louder, and I saw genuine differences in the lives of these new friends. As I read the Bible, the Holy Spirit began to speak to me about a personal relationship with Christ. I had too much pride, though. What would people think? I was just too busy being religious and too stubborn to give in. At least till now.

"But God knew how important it was to get my attention, and he knew just how to do it. One by one, I saw the things that I had used as substitutes either pried out of my hands or lose their significance for me to the point I let go of them. One day I realized I didn't have much left, but I still resisted.

"Last night, when the class met at your home, I was very uncomfortable. Though I knew in my head what the others were talking about, my heart was confused. I went home to bed, but I didn't sleep. I was awake all night. My thoughts were jumbled, but I did some thinking. Could God really love me? Could I possibly have a relationship with him like the other people here last night? Could God possibly understand what I'm going through? I knew I had to talk to someone like you."

"I'm glad you felt that you could come here," I said. "But how did you get my phone number?"

"As soon as the church opened this morning, I called and asked for your number. I knew you would understand. I appreciated so much that you didn't ask me any probing questions, but simply invited me to come right over." She turned and looked out the porch windows. "Oh, the sun is shining. It's so beautiful!"

"The sun was shining when you came in, Laurie, but you didn't notice," I said, smiling.

Her entire countenance had changed. The *Son* indeed had come into her life!

### Reflection

I am glad I didn't put Laurie off that morning because I was "too busy." She probably would never have called back, and I would have lost the opportunity to lead her to Christ.

As 1 Peter 3:15 says, "Always be prepared to give an answer. . . ." Laurie, without knowing it, had made those words a priority in my life that day. I had looked forward to a relaxed morning. I was in the middle of washing my hair and had a big clean-up job left over from the night before. Forty people can cause quite a stir in a house, and there were lots of dishes to do.

If one of my friends had called and asked, "Nellie, how about going out to lunch today?" my answer would have been, "Please give me a rain check. I'm snowed under from the big gang we had over last night."

But Laurie was an emergency. She obviously needed help—now! I felt compelled to drop everything as I was reminded of my commitment to God when I prayed, "Lord, I want to be available to you."

As I continue to read, study, and memorize the Word of God on a daily basis, I am building on my knowledge of that Word. And then witnessing becomes a natural way of life—just as it was for me that day with Laurie.

# 17

## What To Say When . . .

*Someone Asks, "What Do You Think About Homosexuals?"*

### Elizabeth

I was standing on the balcony of the Florida condo that Paul and I had bought for investment or eventual retirement. Paul had been detained by unexpected work, but I didn't mind being by myself for a few days. I love the warmth and the ocean breezes, so I came on ahead.

While looking to see if the beach was crowded, I heard someone call my name. One of my neighbors was trying to get my attention from her balcony across the way.

"Is your husband with you?" she asked.

"Paul had to finish some work, but he'll be down in a couple of days."

"Fred won't be down until next week. How about going out to dinner tonight?"

"Sounds like fun."

I had known Elizabeth casually for a couple of years. We had been introduced by the Delrays, mutual friends and neighbors who were born-again Christians. I knew that Elizabeth had attended their church many times. Jim Delray, who is really up on Revelation, had talked a lot about it to Elizabeth and her husband, Dave. Jim found it fascinating and used it as an opportunity to warn them to be prepared to meet God.

I was pleased when Elizabeth asked me to have dinner with her and prayed for an opening to share the gospel with her. She knew I was a committed Christian and seemed not at all embarrassed when I suggested we say grace before our meal.

We had no sooner started to eat when Elizabeth asked, "Have you met Ed, the new single fellow in your building?"

"I know who he is."

"He's got to be the handsomest man I've ever laid eyes on—" Her voice sort of trailed off before she added, "He's a homosexual, you know."

"No, I didn't know that."

"If I wasn't married and he wasn't gay, I could really go for him," Elizabeth confided.

I didn't know how to respond, so I said nothing until she asked, "Nellie, what do you think about homosexuals?"

"I take the biblical viewpoint," I replied.

"What is that?" She seemed surprised at my answer.

"It's quite clear in the first chapter of Romans and also in the Old Testament that homosexual behavior is an abomination in the eyes of the Lord. He hates it and says that such acts are perversions. I'm committed to love what God loves and hate what he hates."

"Well, then, do you hate Ed?"

"Oh, no. I don't hate Ed—and neither does God—but I hate his lifestyle."

"Would you speak to him if he spoke to you?"

"Of course I would, and I'd be kind to him. God would want me to."

"I didn't know the Bible talked about things like homosexuality," Elizabeth remarked.

"The Bible talks about every aspect of our lives including relationships with other people—children to parents, parents to children, husbands to wives, and wives to husbands. The most important part, of course, is our relationship to God. Would you be interested in knowing what God requires of you to be in his family?"

"Why, yes, I would," she prompted.

"Well, just as Ed has a problem with homosexuality," I continued, "we all have a sin problem. We were all born sinners. We may not be homosexuals, but we haven't been able to live up to God's standard any better than Ed has."

"I understand that," Elizabeth said. "Dave and I hear all the time at church that everyone is a sinner."

"But do you know that God has a remedy for sin?"

"I've never heard it expressed exactly that way. What do you mean by 'remedy'?"

"Well, you know that God is a holy God and refuses to condone any sin. No unrepentant sinner can stand in his presence. In fact, the Bible says in Romans 6:23 that the wages—or the payment—of sin is death. But God has offered each one of us a gift. 'The gift of God is eternal life,' it says in that same verse. I have it here in a booklet if you want to see it," I said, as I opened my purse and pulled out my tool.*

"Oh, yes, I do," said Elizabeth.

I showed her where it was as I continued talking. "But most gifts are given for a reason. God's reason was love, though sin requires punishment and someone has to die. So God chose to die on our behalf. God the Son came into the world to pay the penalty for our sins. That same verse says that God's gift of eternal life is through Jesus Christ our Lord.

"The Bible tells us in Romans 5:8 that God demonstrated his love to us by having Jesus Christ die for us, even while we were still sinners. Jesus is the only way to God because he is the only one who could die for sinners. We cannot get to God by praying to any saint. The saints didn't die for us. Jesus himself said, 'I am the way and the truth and the life. No one comes to the Father except through me.' That's in the Gospel of John—John 14:6."

Elizabeth was very quiet. All she had said as I talked was, "Mmmmm."

"Do you believe the Bible is God's Word?" I asked her.

"Yes, I do. I just don't know it very well."

---

*I feel it is important to keep a tool handy at all times, in my purse or pocket. I can then leave it with the person I am talking to.

There are many booklets available at Christian bookstores, or you may wish to order from publishers. Navigators (Navpress, Box 6000, 3820 N. 30 St, Colorado Springs, CO 80934) has a bridge booklet; Dallas Seminary (3900 Swiss Ave., Dallas, TX 75204) has "How to have a full and meaningful life." "Peace with God" is published by the Billy Graham Evangelistic Association (1300 Harmon Pl., Minneapolis, MN 55403). Other booklets I have used are "Four Spiritual Laws" and "Have You Heard of the Five Jewish Laws?"

Use whatever is comfortable for you and easy to explain. A Bible in a restaurant may be a bit scary until a person realizes it is the book of life.

"Let me read you a couple of verses." I read from John 1:12: " 'Yet to all who received him. . . .' " I paused and looked up. "Jesus," I explained.

She nodded.

" '. . . to those who believed in his name, he gave the right to become children of God.' "

She nodded again.

"Now listen to this one," I went on. " 'For it is by grace you have been saved, through faith—and this is not of yourselves, it is the gift of God—not by works, so that no one can boast.' That's Ephesians 2:8 and 9."

Once again, I heard her say, "Mmmm."

"Now this next verse you're going to have to respond to one way or the other. It's Revelation 3:20. Listen to what Jesus is saying: 'Here I am! I stand at the door and knock. If anyone hears my voice and opens the door, I will come in and eat'—or fellowship—'with him, and he with me.' What he is asking you is, 'Elizabeth, will you open your heart's door to me and let me be involved with you in everything you do? Will you repent of your sins and thank me for dying on the cross for you? Will you ask me to come into your life and make it my home?' "

She looked at me and broke into a smile. "Oh, yes, I want Jesus to come into my life."

"Would you like to tell him that?"

She nodded and we bowed our heads as I led Elizabeth in prayer, she repeated after me: "Thank you for dying on the cross for my sins. And I do want you to come into my life and be my Savior. Amen."

She got up from the table acting like a totally different person. She was excited as she said, "Let's go back to my place. I want to call the Delrays and tell them what happened."

117

As soon as Elizabeth opened the door of her apartment, she headed for the phone. "Come on up, you guys. I've got something exciting to tell you," she told them.

"What's all the excitement about?" Jim asked as he walked in the door.

"This is the first day of the rest of my life. I just asked Jesus Christ to be my Savior."

Of course, the Delrays were delighted.

Later on that evening, Jim got me aside and said, "I've been talking about our faith to Elizabeth for a long time. Why couldn't I lead her to Christ?"

"I don't know, Jim. I know you've been emphasizing the end times, and I'm sure that prepared the way. But she just didn't know how to receive the Lord. You whetted her appetite and made it easy for me to present the gospel to her. We both need to remember that God's timing is always perfect."

Before Elizabeth returned to Florida the following year, she had read the entire Bible through. Then, when Billy Graham had his crusade in Florida, she went forward to let the whole world know she had taken a stand for Jesus Christ.

### Reflection

When God wants us to witness to an individual, he always prepares the way and provides the openings.

I was rather surprised when Elizabeth began to talk in glowing terms about our homosexual neighbor. I didn't know what to say at first. My silence caused her to ask me, "What do you think of homosexuals?"

I had just read the Book of Romans, so I knew exactly what God thought—and I had to speak out and tell her that he hates such perversions.

When Elizabeth found out God's views on homosexuality she wanted to be on the Lord's side. That led naturally to a discussion of sin in general. Then I showed her the Scripture concerning salvation, and she had no argument. Her attitude was: If that's what God wants, that's what I want. It was refreshing.

Jesus said, "Whoever acknowledges me before men, I will also acknowledge him before my Father in heaven" (Matt. 10:32). Notice that when Elizabeth arrived home from our dinner, she immediately went to the phone to tell her friends that she had just been born into the family of God. She was very enthusiastic. Another good sign was that she wanted to go forward at the Billy Graham crusade to publicly identify with Jesus Christ.

It is a constant source of amazement to me to realize that God knows all about us. He knew that I would be in Florida by myself for a few days and that Elizabeth's husband would be detained, too. He knew that both Elizabeth and I would be on the balcony at the same time that morning. Above all, he knew how eager I was to be available to him. So he arranged our divine appointment. What marvelous timing!

# 18

## What To Say When . . .

### *She Says, "I Wish I Knew God Better"*

**The Young Wife**

I was looking at some cosmetics in a department store when the young lady standing next to me turned and said in an excited voice, "Isn't this neat?"

"What is it?" I asked.

"It's nail polish. See, it's a pencil brush and you can carry it in your purse. Should your polish chip, you take your brush out and repair it right on the spot. It dries instantly." She held up the bottle. "It's new on the market and I love it," she added.

"It's a great idea." (I really thought so.)

"Because it's new," the stranger said, "the colors and staying quality aren't very good yet." She was a pretty young woman in her early twenties. Her eyes sparkled. I noticed she was wearing a gold cross with a pearl in the center. Since we had enjoyed our conversation about the nail polish, I felt free to comment on the cross. I had never seen one with a pearl in the center like that.

"What does that cross mean to you?" I asked.

"Oh," she said, "I wear it because I'm Catholic."

"I didn't mean what church you belong to. I meant what does the cross mean to you?"

With a most serene expression on her face, she said, "It reminds me of my Lord."

"That's beautiful."

Then she added wistfully, "I wish I knew God better."

"I can tell you how you can get to know him better," I told her.

"You can?" She looked surprised.

"If you read a portion of the Bible every day, you'll get to know not only what God is like but how much he loves you."

"It's interesting you should mention that. My husband and I were discussing just that very thing this morning. You see, he reads the Bible every day," she explained.

Just then her husband came up and joined us. She told him what we had been discussing, and he seemed pleased. He told me he was from Virginia and that he was raised in a Baptist home. They had been married for only a year and were not attending church anywhere.

I recommended my church to the couple, since it was close to where they had told me they were living. I also gave them my little booklet on the basics of what it means to be a Christian. "Since your husband has had a good Bible background, he'll be able to help you," I told the young woman. He grinned broadly, and they both thanked me as we went our separate ways.

### Reflection

I was glad I had been able to encourage these young people to study the Word together. They were a very handsome couple, but it disturbed me that someone raised in a home where the Bible was such an important part of life—a man who still read it on a daily basis—would marry a woman who knew so little about the Book of Life, despite the cross she wore.

The wife was an exceptionally beautiful girl with a very charming personality. Perhaps in a weak moment her husband had neglected to put God first in his life. Since he was now reading the Bible daily, I thought he might be back on track and hoped his daily example would prompt her to want to know more about the Lord.

Though I could have presented the gospel right then and there, I chose not to. There is a time to press and confront and a time to back off and let the Holy Spirit work. I was prepared to do either, but I depended on the Lord to show me what to do. In this case, I felt that this young woman had someone living with her who could minister to her, now that he was back in fellowship with the Lord.

This experience opened the door for the husband to take the responsibility God intended for him, the role as spiritual head of the house. He had already started to read his Bible again. His wife had noticed that, and they had even had a discussion about it. By not pressing the issue, I simply reminded him that the responsibility for her spiritual growth was his. He appeared delighted, and I am glad that God used me to give that little nudge.

Believers are in Christ, and Christ is in us. Psalm 4:3 tells us that God has set the godly ones apart for himself to delight in. The Gospel of John adds that the only-begotten Son, "who is at the Father's side" (1:18), has declared him and made him known.

We who are in Christ are in the bosom of the Father. When we have our ear close to the heartbeat of the Father, when we are set apart to live to delight him, we can rest in the knowledge that he will minister through us. At times, we may not even realize that our words are falling like hammer blows on someone's heart and conscience, but that's not necessarily for us to know.

We are to trust the Lord to use us and we are to rest in the fact that he will. As we love and speak to those who need new life in Christ, God will give the increase.

# 19

## What To Say When . . .

### They Say, "We Don't Get Much Out of Church. It Seems Dull and Boring"

**Sue and Bill—and Sylvia**

"How are the newlyweds today?" I asked Sue and Bill as we met on our morning walk one day.

"We couldn't be better," Sue said with a smile.

I remember thinking that it was good to see them so happy. Both of them had been married before, Sue had told me earlier. Her husband had been a psychiatrist but had committed suicide. I had also learned that Bill's first wife, on her death bed, had asked her children and husband to come to her room. When they arrived, she started to scream, "Why aren't you praying for me? Can't you see I'm dying?"

Bill had told Sue that his late wife was "a very religious person. Every time there was something going on at church, she was there. If I didn't go with her, she would tell me I was committing a sin. I can't figure out why a religious person would die screaming and yelling. How come no peace?" Sue had no answer, but apparently she thought about it many times.

The next time I met them, Bill addressed me in a very sympathetic tone of voice: "I understand your father is failing rapidly. We're so sorry to hear that. Is he having a hard time?"

"Dad does very well, thank you," I said. "He's really anxious to go home to be with the Lord. He was able to come to the table Thanksgiving Day. We asked him to pray. I'll never forget it. He was very weak. But, when he prayed, his voice was strong and powerful. 'Oh, mighty God,' he prayed, 'You whose eyes circle the earth and keep track of all your children, I thank you for your mercy and lovingkindness all of my life.' "

"That's a beautiful prayer," Bill said. "How old is your father?"

"He's just had his ninety-ninth birthday."

"Remarkable." Bill shook his head in disbelief.

Some time later, after my father finally died, my neighbor Cathy had come to the funeral. When she got home, she told a group of other neighbors, "I just attended the most joyous occasion. It was a funeral. Actually, it was more like a celebration."

The neighbors looked at her as if she were out of her mind. "Joyous funeral? Celebration? I've never heard of such a thing," one of them said.

"Now, hear me out," Cathy had said. "The minister told how he visited Nellie's dad and said to him, 'Ole, the Lord is getting you ready to go home to be with him. Are you afraid?' Now Ole had no strength and no voice left, and he couldn't sit up in bed by himself, but

on his own he sat up and said in a loud voice, 'Nooo!' "
Cathy told me later how amazed the neighbors were.

Soon Sue and Bill had also heard the story, and I shared
a bit more with them since they seemed genuinely interested: "Before Dad died, I heard him pray one day,
'Lord, have mercy on me, an old man, and take me home
to be with you. I love you, Lord Jesus.' Dad could pray
that way because he had a personal relationship with
Jesus Christ."

"What kind of minister did your father have? Who is
he?" Bill asked.

"David Burnham," I said. "He's a man of God who
teaches the truth of the Scripture. He not only teaches
from the Word of God, but he lives it. His gracious spirit
and attitude were a tremendous influence on my father
in the last few years of his life. Why don't you and Sue
attend church with us next Sunday? Then you can hear
for yourself."

"We'd like that very much, and perhaps we can have
dinner together afterwards," Bill suggested. I was excited about their response, and my husband and I prayed
much for them that week.

Bill and Sue really liked the pastor's sermon and
wanted to talk to him after the service. "That's the best
preaching I've ever heard," Bill said. "Why, you're as
good as Billy Graham." Pastor Burnham laughed and
thanked him for his words.

On the way home, Sue was still enthusiastic. "I'd
really like to attend that church. I learned a lot this
morning." To our surprise, Bill added, "I'd like to attend,
too, but not every Sunday. Things come up, you know.
We'll come once in a while though."

I was disappointed and Sue was, too. Later she said to
me, "I'd love to attend church every week, but, since

Bill and I are newlyweds, I'd better be careful not to alienate him. His first wife put such demands on him concerning church activities that he's a bit apprehensive."

"I think you're wise not to push him," I agreed.

Then Sue said, "I'm expecting a friend of mine in a few days and would like you to meet her. She'll be here all week. I don't think Bill will mind if I take her to church. He plans to play golf next Sunday anyway."

"I'd love to meet her," I said. As we parted, I added, "I'd like to stop over tomorrow if you'll be home. I've got something I'd like to share with you."

"I'd like that. Why don't you come over after lunch."

I was a bit nervous as I knocked on Sue's door the next day. Maybe it was excitement I felt. I had been praying for Sue's salvation for some time and felt that today would be a good time to talk to her about the Lord.

"Come on in," she said. "I want you to meet my friend Sylvia. She arrived two days' earlier than I expected. We've already had a chance to talk and catch up on things." Sylvia was very friendly and had a beautiful smile. I liked her instantly. After a few minutes of small talk, I prepared to leave.

"Didn't you say you had something to share with me?" Sue asked.

"I'll wait until your company leaves," I said, not wanting to put her on the spot until we were alone.

"Oh, Sylvia is such a good friend of mine that I don't mind if she hears what you have to say. I'm anxious to hear it myself."

"Well," I hesitated, "you seemed to be so interested in our pastor's message that I wanted to be sure you knew how to be in the family of God."

Sue and Sylvia both looked at me in disbelief. "You

won't believe what we've just been talking about," Sue said. "I was just telling Sylvia that I was happy in my marriage and had enough money to live comfortably, but there's something missing in my life. I told her I think my problem is spiritual. Sylvia feels her problem is spiritual, too, and then you knocked on the door. It's absolutely amazing!"

I thought, *Amazing, yes, but it's God's timing.*

Sylvia said, "We've both attended church most of our lives, but we don't get much out of it. It seems dull and boring."

"Having a relationship with Jesus Christ is anything but boring," I said. "You see, he came to give us abundant life. He speaks to us through his Word, the Bible, and we speak to him through prayer. It's really very exciting."

"Oh, I believe in Jesus, but I don't know the Bible very well," Sylvia said.

"But believing facts about him can be like knowing facts of history that don't really affect the heart. A personal relationship with Jesus Christ involves a commitment to him. It involves admitting that we are sinners who need a Savior, sinners who cannot save ourselves. It means repenting of our sins and receiving Christ as our Savior."

I opened my purse and took out my Bible, turning to Romans 6:23. "The Bible says that 'the wages of sin is death'—we deserve to die because we're sinners—'but the gift of God is eternal life in Christ Jesus our Lord.' He died the death we deserve for being such sinners. He actually became our substitute. John 3:16 says, 'For God so loved the world that he gave his one and only Son, that whoever believes in him shall not perish but have eternal life.' "

Tears came as both Sue and Sylvia admitted they were sinners and that they needed Christ as their Savior. We prayed together and each one asked the Lord to come into her life.

"It's strange," Sylvia said. "I feel like a new person, like a load is off my back." Joy had replaced her tears.

Sylvia left for home a couple of days later, and we helped her find a good Bible-teaching church in her area. Sue and I began having Bible studies together. Her desire to learn was delightful and refreshing.

About that time, Bill developed a severe eye infection and was extremely concerned about it. "Please ask the people at your church to pray for me," he said. "If my eye gets better, I'll start coming to church."

"You can't bargain with God," I replied. "You serve him because you love him, not to get his favor. But of course, I *will* ask our church members to pray for your physical and spiritual healing."

Bill's eye got better, but he didn't come to church.

Some time after that, he and Sue went on a trip. They were to be gone for several months. As they were leaving, Bill promised me, "Things will be different when we return. I'll start coming to church."

That never happened. I later got a card from Sue saying, "I have sad news. Bill passed away in his sleep."

### Reflection

Sue and Sylvia were honest about their spiritual condition and responded to the work of the Holy Spirit in their hearts.

Bill, on the other hand, wanted God's benefits with no strings attached. He had the witness of my father who died triumphantly, the witness of Sue's conversion,

129

the witness of his own healing as the probable result of prayer, and the witness I gave him. Though God had answered his questions about life and death time after time, Bill never saw the truth.

We can never fully know what is in another's heart—the condition of the soil upon which our seed will fall. But our responsibility is to sow nonetheless, trusting in God that we have sowed "good seed." It is to be our hope that the Lord's timing will allow the seed to root in fertile soil, so that the person to whom we witness will hear and understand the Word. (Read Matthew 13.)

Though we can never know what tomorrow will bring, anyone "who knows the good" must do it. (Read James 4:13–17.)

# 20

## What To Say When . . .

### *He Says, "We Live Together; I Like to Try the Merchandise Before I Buy"*

**The Anonymous Couple**

All sorts of interesting things happen when I take walks in my neighborhood. It's a great way to get acquainted, and I often manage to get a word in here and there about the Lord. I don't plan it that way, but the opportunities are always there—whether they result in a person's salvation or are merely a reminder to others that God loves them and is keenly interested in what they do.

One such morning I noticed a very attractively dressed couple walking in front of me about a half-block away. When I caught up with them, I said, "What beautiful outfits you're wearing. They're so well coordinated." She had on a tan and brown outfit and his was a deep-gold velour walking suit.

I looked at the woman, who was probably in her fifties, and said, "I bet you bought your husband the suit he's wearing."

The man turned to me and said, "She's not my wife; she's my girlfriend."

"Oh, I'm sorry. I guess I shouldn't take such things for granted," I apologized.

"Lots of people make that mistake," he told me. "You see, we live together; I like to try the merchandise before I buy."

"Oh, I'm disappointed," I said.

"Why?"

"God doesn't approve of that sort of arrangement. He says so in his Word."

The woman looked chagrined. "I was raised on the Word," she said, "and I should know better. I know you're right."

The man looked at her in surprise. He repeated, "I like to try the merchandise before I buy."

"And, if you don't like it, you discard it?" I asked.

He just shrugged his shoulders.

"I should know better. I was raised on the Word," she said again as they walked away.

### Reflection

I had no idea when I saw this couple walking in front of me that I would say anything but a complimentary word about their appearance, but once again God nudged me when the opportunity afforded itself. I took a stand for his righteousness, telling these two people gently but firmly that God would not approve of their living together.

My witness was a reminder to the woman that disobedience to God's Word doesn't bring any real happiness, but only misery in the end.

The man didn't seem to know what I was talking about. As they left, I hoped they would discuss what I had said. It was up to her to explain. And it was up to her to respond to the claims of God on her life.

I felt no liberty at the time to press her for repentance and a change in her life. Had she come to me alone for help, of course I would have. But had I confronted her at this time, I would have embarrassed her in front of this man and probably angered both of them.

It is important to remember that the cross—not the witnessing—must be the offensive weapon against sin. When we anger the person we are witnessing to, we build resentment, so we must be gentle and solicitous. We want the person's best good and must never add cement to the wall anyone has thrown up against the Lord.

Everywhere we go, we are to bring the light of the Word. We are to take a stand for righteousness, even if it means we speak out against sin. But I can't emphasize enough that we must do this with love and sensitivity, allowing the message of the cross to reach another's heart in whatever way God chooses.

# 21

## What To Say When . . .

### *She Says, "My Family Didn't Place Much Importance on Jesus Christ"*

**Marge**

We were sunning ourselves. Marge sat on a lounge chair next to mine, beside the pool of our place in Florida.

"Did you see the TV presentation "Peter and Paul" last night?" she asked.

"I saw only part of it," I said.

"Well, it interested me—very much. I saw a film about the resurrection a couple of years ago, and I learned things about Jesus Christ I never knew before. Since then, he's held a greater place in my life than ever before."

"What's your religious background, Marge?"

"Oh, I was raised in a Christian Science home, and my family didn't place much importance on Jesus Christ. I've been searching for something better ever since.

Sometimes I think I'm close, but then I feel as though I'm knocking my head against a stone wall." She turned to me. "What about you? Did you have a religious upbringing?"

"I was raised in a Christian home," I told her, "and attended a church where the Bible was taught as the Word of God. I read and memorized portions of Scripture many times out of a sense of duty." I turned my head so I could get more direct sun on the other side of my face. "Then I began to realize that I was virtually sitting on a gold mine. I had the words of eternal life at my fingertips, but I wasn't sharing them with anyone. I told God that I wanted to be available to serve him. Now I have a Bible study group made up of women from various religious backgrounds. Many of these women really have no idea why Christ came to earth or why he had to die—or even how we can become a member of the family of God."

I hesitated just a moment and added, "I sense you have a heart to know God. You say you're bumping your head against a stone wall. You need a breakthrough. I believe I can help you if you're interested."

"Oh, I most certainly am interested." Marge's face showed me how determined she was. We made a date to meet the following day.

When I arrived at her apartment, Marge was full of questions: "Tell me more about Jesus Christ. Who exactly is he? Why is he so important?"

"Well, Marge, Jesus Christ is God. He came in the flesh so that we might know what God the Father is like. He actually came to give us salvation. You see, we can't save ourselves or make ourselves acceptable to God except through Jesus Christ. He died on the cross for our sins. We deserved to die, but he willingly took our place. It seems inconceivable to think that anyone would be willing to take the punishment for my sins, but that's how great God's love is."

She stopped me. "I've been raised to believe there is no sin, but only human error. I've never been taught the need for a Savior."

"I don't think we need to be persuaded that sin is a reality," I said. "The papers report it daily, and we only need to look into our own hearts to know it exists."

We read John 10:10 together and discussed how Jesus came to give us life, the very best of life, the abundant life. Then we read Revelation 3:20, where Jesus is standing at our heart's door, knocking, desiring entrance into our lives. I told Marge, "But he won't force himself in. He only comes by invitation. Marge, is there any reason why you don't want to receive Christ as your Savior?"

She looked at me expectantly and said, "I do want to invite Jesus Christ into my life as Savior and Lord."

I prayed and then she prayed, "Dear Lord, Thank you for guiding us to buy an apartment in this complex, so that Nellie and I could meet and that through her you could bring me salvation. Thank you for coming to give me abundant life. I don't deserve it. I'm a sinner and need you to save me. Thank you for dying on the cross and for taking the punishment I should have. I receive you as my Savior. Thank you, Lord."

### Reflection

Marge made it easy for me. Here was an opportunity staring me in the face, begging to be taken. I could not walk away from it.

When people have been brought up in a cultist religion, their hearts are often too hard for the Spirit of God to touch. But Marge said she had been searching for truth and had mentioned the television special about Peter and Paul. She asked me what my religious background was. In effect, she initiated the conversation and turned it to spiritual things herself.

I correctly sensed that the Lord had already prepared Marge's heart. I brought in the John 10:10 verse to show her that Jesus came to earth to give her the abundant life she had been seeking, the "something better" she mentioned.

We do have something better: God's gift of eternal life!

# 22

## What To Say When . . .

### *He Says, "We Won't Have Peace Until Messiah Comes"*

**George**

He rolled his eyes and made a face and then looked directly at me. I had done nothing to trigger this stranger's hostility and wondered what the problem was. I was standing behind him in line at the drugstore as he stared at me, apparently waiting for me to say something.

I smiled and asked, "What's the problem?"

The man pointed to the woman standing in front of him at the checkout counter. I noticed she was having a hard time getting the loose change from the bottom of her purse. When she finally paid her bill and left, he again turned to me with the same impatient look. "I would think people would get themselves together before they go shopping," he said in disgust.

"I agree," I said. "It is a bit annoying at times when people take forever to get a bit of change from the bottom of a large, already packed purse. But who knows what else that woman is carrying. Perhaps a broken heart?" Then, with a twinkle in my eyes, I said, "Maybe you could learn something from this experience."

"What?"

"Patience."

"Oh, I've got plenty of that," he said.

I couldn't help but chuckle to myself. Then I said, "The Bible says tribulation works patience."

The man waited for me to pay my bill and followed me outside. He seemed to want to continue the conversation. He told me his name was George, then he added, "You know, you remind me of my aunt. She's going to be eighty years old next week."

"Thanks a lot! Do I really look that old?"

"No. What I mean is—she talks like you. She's joined some kind of Christian cult, but she's okay. We're going to have a big birthday party for her."

"My dad's going to be ninety-eight in November," I said.

"Wow! Is he in his right mind?"

"Oh, yes," I answered, "he's in great shape and takes long walks every day. And he loves people. One thing I'll always be grateful for is the influence he's had on my life. When I grew up, I remember my dad getting up at five o'clock to read the Scriptures before he went to work."

"I'm not one for reading the Scriptures," George said, "but I do go to temple once in a while."

"Oh, you're Jewish. I've got lots of Jewish friends, including a rabbi friend in Florida. The Jews are really a special people, since they're God's chosen ones."

George looked at me with a smile and said, "Some people would ask, 'Chosen for what?' "

I smiled. "God didn't choose the Jews because they were especially great, but because he loved them and chose them in particular to carry the promise of the Messiah and to tell the Gentiles what he is like. But I think it's reversed these days. I, a Gentile, must tell the Jew what God is like."

"Mmmmm," he said, "but we won't have peace until Messiah comes."

"You're right about that. But he's already come once and is coming again, just like you said. I believe Jesus Christ is the promised Messiah."

I opened my purse and took out my little booklet and said, "Why don't you read this and then ask your aunt what she thinks of it."

"Thanks," George said. "I guess everyone should have something to believe in, but not be pushed into anything."

"I couldn't agree with you more," I nodded. "But it's fun to talk about it, isn't it?"

"Sure is. I'm a salesperson. I like to talk."

"I'm a bit of a salesperson myself," I said. "I like to sell people on God. You see, I'd like to see the Jewish people get back to the Scriptures and see the fantastic heritage they have."

He asked me my full name and told me his. Then he put out his hand and said, "It sure was nice talking to you."


### Reflection

I don't talk to everyone I meet in the same way. (Someone else might have told me off if I talked to him like this.) Because I'm available to the Lord, I feel free to speak for him, and he gives me discernment. I feel my way along and go as far as I can. The other person's behavior often gives me the cue. George felt free to criticize the customer in front of him and let me know how he felt. That gave me the opener. I was free to criticize him genially and chide him about not having patience. Then I was able to insert a Bible verse and direct the conversation along more eternal lines.

This man was obviously not ready to talk deeply about spiritual things, so I didn't push him. Some sow and some water. So I pray that George will think about our talk and read the booklet. Perhaps someone else will come along and do the watering. It takes a lot of people to do God's work. How great to have a little share in it!

# 23

## What To Say When . . .

### She Says, "I'm a Very Confused Person. They Tell Me I'm Manic Depressive"

**Yvonne**

I knew that woman in the audience didn't like me. I could tell by her body language. She sat with her arms folded and had a hostile look on her face. She might as well have worn a sign that said, "What do you think you can teach me that I don't know already?"

I had accepted an invitation to hold a series of morning Bible classes at a church on the east side of our city, about thirty miles away. Since this was the first women's Bible class they had had, I was excited. Our study would be in the Book of Galatians.

When I arrived, I was surprised to see men in the audience. "I thought this was a women's Bible class," I said to Edith, my hostess. "I didn't know there would be any men here. And they look so serious!"

"They're just deacons," she told me.

"Mmmm, I bet they're checking me out. I really don't blame them. After all, I'm a Baptist and this is a Lutheran church."

Edith laughed as she patted my shoulder. "Don't worry."

I wasn't worried, but I did feel somewhat uneasy. I wanted to be a blessing to these women, so I prayed and asked God to break down any barrier that might stand in the way.

After I was introduced, I began by saying, "I'm not a theologian. I'm a homemaker who has had good Bible teaching all my life, and I love to study and share the Scriptures. I hope we will all learn from each other as we study the Book of Galatians together."

I spoke for half an hour on the first chapter, contrasting the pure gospel of Jesus Christ with "a different gospel—which is really no gospel at all" (Gal. 1:6). The Galatians were trying to add to the gospel by putting unnecessary burdens on believers. I mentioned the importance of being biblical and not accepting "every wind of teaching" that came along (Eph. 4:14).

That was the problem in Galatia, I said. I referred to the Bereans, who had received the message with eagerness but "examined the Scriptures every day to see if what Paul said was true" (Acts 17:11). I also brought out the point that in Paul's greeting he said, "Grace and peace to you . . ." not "peace and grace" (Gal. 1:3). We first have to experience God's grace before we can have his peace.

We then had a coffee break. After that there were to be questions and a discussion. During the break, one of the deacons came up, put his two hands on mine, and said, "Lady, you've got it all together!" What a relief! The barrier was broken.

Standing behind the deacon, a woman waited patiently to speak to me. She was the one who had sat, arms folded, with a "show me" look on her face. She introduced herself as "Yvonne" and asked, "Would you be willing to talk to me after the meeting is over? I need help in several areas of my life."

I was amazed. Sweetness and humility had replaced her hostility. Her attitude had completely changed.

When we talked later, Yvonne said, "I'm a very confused person. I've gone to church for years, but I don't think I've experienced God's grace like you talked about this morning. I know because I don't have peace."

I looked at this attractive, well-groomed woman and wondered what her problem might be, since she seemed outwardly composed. She said, "I'm a teacher, but I'm having problems keeping my job. I sometimes go into deep depression and have had to be hospitalized several times. They tell me I'm manic depressive."

Disturbing thoughts flooded my mind. She needed a doctor. I was not equipped to handle this.

Then she went on. "I have highs and lows. I go on spending sprees that are very exciting. But, when I can't pay my bills, I get very depressed and anxious. I try to borrow money and that makes me feel worse. I like beautiful things and want to look as nice as the other women in this group, but I feel like a nothing compared to them. You might say that I have a poor self-image. I don't feel accepted. I hear about the abundant life that Christ came to give, but I certainly don't have an abundance. I'm always struggling to pay my bills. Can you help me?"

"Well, first of all," I said, "the abundant life does not

mean an abundance of things. It means a life full of joy and peace and contentment. When we recognize the fact that Jesus died for our sins, took our place on the cross and paid our penalty, we have an overwhelming desire to commit ourselves to him. When we do that, we realize we are free from guilt and the awful burden of sin. Then and only then can we understand what the abundant life is all about."

"Then what is grace all about?" Yvonne asked.

"Grace means unmerited favor. We can't get Brownie points from God by doing good deeds or by trying to turn over a new leaf without his help. Ephesians 2:8 and 9 says, 'For it is by grace you have been saved, through faith—and this not from yourselves, it is the gift of God—not by works, so that no one can boast.' We need to understand that God is holy and that everything he does is right. Sin is completely offensive to him. We all have offended our Holy God.

"The good news is that God loves us and demonstrated this by sending his Son, Jesus Christ, to die for us. He didn't do this for so-called good people, for 'while we were still sinners, Christ died for us.' That's in Romans 5:8. In the light of this, all we need do to be accepted by God is to confess that we are sinners and want to receive Jesus Christ as our personal Savior. He paid the penalty for our sins. Then God not only forgives us; he accepts us into his family."

Yvonne shook her head. "I've never done that—that is, confessed my sins. And I haven't received Jesus as my Savior. I always thought the important thing was to attend church on Sundays."

"Oh, it's important to attend church and to be with other believers," I agreed, "but the most important issue of all is acknowledging Jesus as your Savior from sin.

You need to invite him into your life. Unless you do, you'll be separated from God forever. When you commit your life to him, you will experience peace and can begin a brand-new life. It's called being born again."

"I really need to do that," Yvonne said as she bowed her head and began to pray: "Dear God, I know I sin. I think it's the cause of all of my problems. I think it's wrong of me to buy perfume I can't afford and expensive clothes I can't pay for. That's why I'm so miserable and don't have peace. I confess this and the other sins I've committed, and I receive Jesus as my Savior. Thank you for dying on the cross for me and for giving me a way out of my misery."

When she looked up, she smiled shyly and said, "With God's help, I'm going to lick this problem. I really want to."

During the discussion period the next week, Yvonne stood up and said, "Today, I can say for sure that I am a Christian. I don't just try to do Christian things. Our lesson today says that we are not justified or saved by keeping the law or by doing good things, but by placing our faith in Jesus Christ. I placed my faith in Jesus last week after class, and I'm beginning to understand what is meant by the abundant life. It's not an abundance of things but an abundance of peace. Today I can truthfully say that I have peace."

The following week, Yvonne showed me a budget she had made for herself and told me, "I thought you would like to know that I'm working on my priorities. I made a list of things I thought I needed. Then I crossed off the things I couldn't afford. The surprising thing was discovering that the items I crossed off weren't *needed* at all. They were only things I *wanted.*

"I feel so good about it. I believe God is helping me

to get my life under control. I'm so much more relaxed, and I have a peace that I never experienced before. Another thing that is helping me out of my confusion is reading small portions of Scripture and thinking about them."

I agreed with her. "It's good to hide God's Word in our hearts," I said. "The Bible says it keeps us from sinning. Psalm 119:11 says, 'I have hidden your word in my heart that I might not sin against you.' "

Each week Yvonne had something new to share about the working of the Spirit of God in her life. It was interesting to watch her growth as the weeks passed. As we studied the fifth chapter of Galatians, concerning the acts of the sinful nature in contrast to the fruit of the Spirit, it was obvious that Yvonne was aware of the transformation taking place in her life. She was a joy to behold and a cause of praise to the Father.

When the women ended the series of Bible studies with a luncheon, I asked Edith, our hostess, "Would you allow Yvonne to tell the group about her new job? I think it will mean a lot to her." I also knew that everyone was deeply interested in the change that had taken place from week to week right in front of their eyes.

Yvonne spoke about working the past month for a company that sends out representatives to help women with their grooming. "I show them how to fix their nails and hair and how to choose clothes and the proper accessories. Some women don't know where to start and just need a little direction. I give them low-cost, budget-conscious tips for self-improvement. My job is to make a completely new person out of each one of them, at least on the outside."

While she was talking, I couldn't help but think of the transformation in Yvonne's life. The dark clouds were gone from her face. Instead, there was a beautiful smile and a confidence that God had given her. I was excited for her and thanked God for allowing me to witness the change, as she continued her story:

"I just finished with a woman who was very happy with her new appearance. I told her, 'I've done the best I can to make you look beautiful and I think you do. I've completed my part, but there is another part of you that needs changing before we can say we're done.'

"My client looked puzzled. 'What is that?' she asked.

"'That is something only God can do,' I told her. Then I said, 'Let me tell you how God changed me from the inside and how it affected the outside of my life.' "

What an ending to our Bible-study series! I wanted to give Yvonne a standing ovation. Instead, I sat there and cried tears of joy.

Even though Yvonne lives a distance away, I have seen her several times in the past years. The last time I talked to her on the phone she was still growing as a believer.

"When I first met you," she said, "I was full of fear and mistrust. I felt anxious and frightened, though I may have looked hostile. I really looked up to you as a role model and came for help. I was seeking and searching, and God has taught me to replace fear with love. He has brought me peace and helped me forgive those I once mistrusted. I'm learning so much and have a lot more to learn. I have so much to thank God for."

### Reflection

Yvonne came to Christ when the Word of God was explained to her. I added verses of Scripture to my conversation, letting the Holy Spirit use them and work in her heart.

I was wrong to judge her attitude initially by body language and facial expression. Man looks on the outward appearance, but God looks on the heart. Looks are deceiving and often cause us to make wrong judgments. Our job is to be faithful and not put up barriers between ourselves and the person to whom God wants us to witness.

We must also have full confidence that God will use his Word in people's hearts. Yvonne picked up on the salutation of Paul and the little lesson I drew from it— that we must first experience grace before we can have peace. That hit her problem head-on and drew her to the Savior. I had no way of knowing that God would use that little truth to bring Yvonne to himself. How important for us to be full of the word and full of trust that the Holy Spirit will bring people to Christ by using the little things that spill from our lips.

And talk about fulfillment! What perfect joy it is to see one whom we have pointed to the Savior in her turn point someone else to him. Yvonne did this and, to my knowledge, is still winning others.

# 24

## What To Say When . . .

### She Says, "I Have a Problem—I Don't Know How to Pray"

**Evelyn**

My husband and I always look forward to September, the time of year we visit our married daughters in New England. Greta lives in Connecticut and Karen in Massachusetts. En route, we usually stop at Rockport, a quaint little Massachusetts town nestled by the ocean. We stay at a favorite motel, which has all the facilities we enjoy—tennis courts, a swimming pool, a sauna and whirlpool tub.

One year, during our annual stopover, I decided to swim after a game of tennis with Paul. He chose to sit on the pool deck and catch up on his reading—a choice that would play an important part in the incident that followed.

I was feeling so refreshed and relaxed by the water

and so caught up in my own little world that I barely noticed the one other person—a woman—in the pool. She appeared to be enjoying her swim just as much as I. Eventually we got close enough to speak to each other, and she introduced herself.

"Hi, I'm Evelyn," she said.

"Hi, I'm Nellie Pickard."

"Where are you from?"

"I'm from Michigan. My husband and I are out here visiting our daughters. Where do you live?"

"Oh, I live in Essex, just a few miles from here."

I wondered what she was doing in a motel so close to home; and, of course, with my innate curiosity I couldn't resist asking her.

"I recently injured my back," she said, "and my doctor prescribed swimming and the whirlpool to strengthen my muscles. I have an arrangement with the motel management, and for a yearly fee they let me swim here whenever I want. Unfortunately, I missed Sunday and Monday and can really feel the difference."

"I suppose you went to church on Sunday and did your housework on Monday and got your back out of whack again," I prompted.

"Oh, no, I didn't go to church on Sunday. In fact," she said, "I have a problem—I don't know how to pray."

Now why would someone say to a perfect stranger, "I don't know how to pray"? I was immediately aware that this was one of God's divine appointments for me. Right there in that swimming pool, he had arranged an opportunity for me to share my faith with Evelyn. I've learned over the years that effective witnessing involves being alert, responsive, and sensitive to the people I meet—even in swimming pools. It also means looking for "openers" that will help me make a smooth connection to share the love of Christ. Evelyn had given me a fantastic opener. I could hardly believe it. She even repeated it: "I just don't know how to pray. I try, but it just seems to hit the ceiling."

"Perhaps I can help you," I said. "I teach a women's Bible class, and I often meet women who don't know how to pray. I might even be able to tell you what your problem really is."

"How can you possibly tell me what my problem is?" she asked. "We've only known each other for a few minutes."

"Tell me, Evelyn, when you pray, do you go directly to God?"

"Of course."

"That's your problem," I said. "You see, God demands perfection. We can't approach him in our imperfect condition (*see* Reflection, p. 154). We need a mediator (1 Tim. 2:5; John 4:6)."

"Well," she said, "I keep the Ten Commandments, and I'm really good to my neighbors."

I responded very kindly, "You look like such a nice person, and I'll bet you *are* good to your neighbors. But, you see, no one has kept the commandments perfectly. God's Word says, 'All have sinned and come short of the glory of God.' God demands perfection, so that's your problem."

I wasn't sure how she would accept this truth but she asked anxiously, "What in the world can I do?"

"Fortunately, God didn't leave us to flounder," I said. "He provided a way. He came to earth himself to die for our sins and in our place. The Bible says that the Lord Jesus is standing at your heart's door, knocking and desiring that you will open the door of your life, repent of your sins, and receive him as your Savior."

"I had a maid," Evelyn said, "who tried to tell me about Jesus Christ many times. Because she was my maid, I didn't pay much attention. Now you're telling me some of the same things."

Usually, when witnessing, I take out copies of a little booklet that presents the plan of salvation in a simple, precise manner. With the other person following along, I read it aloud. I have found this an important tool that has been invaluable to me in many situations. It also gives the person I'm talking with a chance to look away from me for a while. A change of eye contact allows a more relaxed feeling. Then I give the book to the person to keep. However, here I was standing in a swimming pool with no booklets!

We decided to go to the whirlpool and continue our conversation there. On the way, I stopped by Paul and asked him to please go and get me two copies of the booklet. God had *him* there for a purpose, too! When Paul brought them, I gave one to Evelyn and invited her to follow along as I read aloud. As I finished, I confronted her with a direct question: "Is Christ running your life—or are you?"

"I've definitely been running my life," she said.

"Do you want to continue to run your life? Or would you like Jesus Christ to come into your life and take control?" I held my breath, praying that her answer would be yes.

"I would very much like Christ to come into my life and take over," she said. "How can I tell him that?"

I explained that God looks at the heart and is not concerned with the specific words we say, and then I helped her pray. Right there in the whirlpool with the warm, soothing water swirling around us, Evelyn joyously received Christ as her Savior.

I told her that it was important that she tell someone that she had accepted Christ as her Savior, as a means of reaffirming her faith and sharing it with someone else. "I have a friend named Julie Kerr," I said, "who lives in Hamilton, about twenty miles away from here, and she's a Christian. It would be good for you to tell her of your experience."

"I know her!" Evelyn laughed. "She sells real estate and showed me some houses just two weeks ago. My husband and I buy homes that need fixing and then sell them."

Neither of us said, "It's a small world," but I'm sure we both thought it. If I ever doubted that God has pre-arranged appointments for me, my doubts vanished right then and there.

Evelyn returned to the pool to finish her workout. I watched her as she glided through the water effortlessly. When she was finished, she said happily, "I prayed every stroke of the way."

I smiled. "I thought you didn't know how to pray."

"I didn't, but I do now!" She was radiant.

Over the years, I have kept in touch with Evelyn by letters and phone calls and have had the privilege and joy of seeing her grow as a Christian.


### Reflection

Evelyn is just one example of how opportunities for witnessing occur everywhere. Sometimes, as she did, a person will begin the conversation; other times, I have to ask a question or make a comment to get things going. I use something that is available and would obviously be of interest to both of us.

In Evelyn's case, I was able to attract her attention

with the protocol of prayer. She found it difficult to understand why she couldn't go to God except through Christ. That offered an excellent opportunity to explain to her that God is holy and demands perfection. Since we are not holy, we cannot approach Holy God in and of ourselves, any more than we can on a human level walk directly into the President's office.

When a person tells me, "I have a problem, I don't know how to pray" or "I try to pray and I feel as though my prayers hit the ceiling," I can usually identify their problem.

If I start out by saying, "You can come to God only as a repentant sinner," he or she would become defensive. We need to know that no one can reach God's standard (Rom. 3:23). God's standard is perfection.

Evelyn knew she could not keep God's commands—perfectly—and immediately asked, "What can I do?" That is what I was waiting for.

I was then able to tell her that the Lord Jesus Christ is the answer to that dilemma. When we accept him as our Savior, we can come to God in his name—we are clothed in his righteousness, and now God the Father will hear us.

I use John 14:13–14, where Jesus says, "And I will do whatever you ask *in my name,* so that the Son may bring glory to the Father. You may ask me for anything, *in my name* and I will do it." Or I might also use Jesus' words in John 16:23: ". . . I tell you the truth, my Father will give you whatever you ask *in my name.*"

"In my name" means all that Christ's character stands for. We receive an answer to our requests because we ask according to his righteousness. Of course, we must not be careless about praying to our heavenly Father in the name of the Lord Jesus and in the power of the Holy Spirit (Jude 20).

Last year, while attending a Bible study in Massachusetts with my daughter Karen, I saw a little slip of a woman who caught my attention. We looked at each other and our eyes locked in recognition.

"Evelyn!"

"Nellie!" We both spoke at once.

We hadn't seen each other in several years, and that was in the swimming pool. We both looked different in street clothes.

What a time we had catching up! Evelyn was so excited about the things she was learning. "Nellie," she said, "I'm trying to make up for lost time. I attend two Bible studies every week. I have so much to learn. Oh, how I wish I hadn't wasted so much time. All my life I've been attending Unity and it was such a waste. I didn't learn about the Bible at all."

We sat together in class, and I told everyone about our meeting in the swimming pool several years before, when Evelyn had come to know Christ. What a difference salvation makes in a life!

# 25

## What To Say When . . .

### *She Says, "I'm Searching . . . but I Don't Think I've Found Him Yet"*

**Mary Beth**

I was sitting in the overflow room of our church one Sunday when I noticed a young woman coming in to take a chair. I smiled at her and she smiled back. Then I saw her take a visitor's brochure from an usher as my husband whispered to me, "You be sure to talk to her."

I slipped over to the newcomer and introduced myself. I said, "Visitors are invited to the library for a cup of coffee after the service and an opportunity to meet the church staff. I hope you'll come. It's a good place to get acquainted. I'd like to meet you there."

"I'd love to," she whispered, after telling me her name was Mary Beth.

When she came into the library, I asked her, "Do you

live in the area, and have you ever visited our church before?"

"I live nearby, but I've never attended your church. I'm not too happy with the church I belong to. I just don't get anything out of it. I asked the boy I ride to school with if he knew of a good church. He said Highland Park Baptist was a good church."

"Does your friend attend this church?" I asked.

"Oh, no. He isn't interested in religion."

I found that amusing and asked, "Tell me, are you a full-time student or do you work?"

"I attend Wayne State University, but I have Fridays off," she told me.

"How about having lunch with me on Friday? Then I'll tell you about our church and the young people's activities and anything else you'd like to know."

"Sounds like fun. Give me directions to your house, and I'll be there."

When Mary Beth arrived on Friday, I felt as though I was welcoming one of my own children. She greeted me with a big smile and a hug. As we enjoyed our lunch together, I asked, "Do you have any brothers and sisters?"

"Lots," she said, laughing. "There are eleven children in our family. My father is a doctor, and he and my mom have taken good care of us. One of my brothers is an attorney, and I have a sister who goes to law school." Mary Beth seemed proud of her family, and I enjoyed hearing about them.

Then she said, "I have another sister and brother-in-law who were invited to a Christian businessmen's meeting and there they found the Lord. Their lives are so different since they've—" she hesitated—"found the Lord. They're so happy. I wish everybody could find the Lord. The world would be a better place to live in."

158

"Have you found the Lord, Mary Beth?" I asked.

"I'm searching, and I know about him, but I don't think I've found him yet."

"It's not enough to know about him," I said. "We need to confess that we have sinned against him and need his cleansing and forgiveness. We need to receive him as our Savior. Knowing about the Lord is a matter of the head. Receiving him is a matter of the heart. It's a commitment to him and becomes a relationship. We then become a member of the family of God. Look what it says here in the Bible—"

I turned to Revelation 3:20 and explained, "You see, Jesus is waiting for you to invite him into your life. Is there any reason why you wouldn't want to ask him to be your Savior and Lord?"

To my delight she said with a big smile, "Not a reason in the world."

We bowed our heads and Mary Beth prayed, "Lord, I know that I'm a sinner. Never before have I invited you to take charge of my life. I ask your forgiveness. I now ask you to be my Savior and to take control of my life."

When she looked up, her face was radiant. "I'm so glad I took this step today," she said. Tears filled her eyes. When she left, she hugged me again and said, "I'll see you on Sunday."

Mary Beth and I have had Bible study together since then, and she attended the college-age Sunday-school class the very next Sunday. I took her to the room and introduced her to the members, suggesting that she tell everyone what had happened to her the previous Friday.

"I asked Jesus Christ to come into my life," she said.

The class hadn't expected to hear that and said in unison, "Ahhhhhh!"

## Reflection

Look around. You never know who is sitting next to you in church. Just because a visitor is all dressed up and sits listening attentively to the sermon is no reason to believe she or he is saved. Mary Beth was a person whose heart was ready. Her sister and brother-in-law had done the sowing and watering. Their happy lives had proved to her the reality of salvation. All I did was give Mary Beth a nudge.

Again, let me say that it's important to use our homes for witnessing. If you open the door and invite these very needy people in, you are showing them that you are interested and available. In 1 Peter 4:9 we are admonished to practice hospitality. It pleases the Lord—and we get the blessing.

# 26

## What To Say When . . .

### *She Says, "Shut Up!"*

**Penny and Her Family**

"I believe we have a couple of newcomers in our class today," I said during a women's Bible study I was leading. "Let's take a few minutes to get acquainted before we get into the lesson. Each of you tell two things about yourself. If this is your first time here, tell us what circumstances brought you."

I was especially interested in a tall, blonde woman who came by herself, but I didn't have a chance to speak to her before class except to nod and smile. "My name's Penny Wilson," she said when it was her turn. "A woman in our car pool invited me to come. I'm really concerned about the drug situation in the public schools, so I put my children in a private school. Since my husband isn't willing to pay any of the tuition, I'm working in my home as a hairdresser to pay for their schooling."

I decided I wanted to know more about this industrious young woman. I also wondered what her religious background was and watched for little clues as I taught. She seemed tense. She listened but never volunteered to answer any questions.

After the third week, Penny was a bit more relaxed, and I was delighted when she spoke up in class: "Would it be all right if I brought my sister-in-law to class? I think this is what she needs. You see, she has an incurable disease and needs something that will give her peace." She turned and looked at the others in the group. "Don't misunderstand me. She's deeply religious, but she doesn't have what you have."

"We encourage all of you to bring your friends to our class," I said.

*Things are unfolding,* I thought. Penny was concerned about her sister-in-law, but I was concerned about Penny. I didn't like the way she said, "She doesn't have what *you* have," so I asked the Lord to give me wisdom to know how to handle the situation. Though I didn't want to rush things, neither should I wait too long to speak. I asked God to let his Word work in her heart.

The next week, Penny brought both her mother and sister-in-law to class. We were studying the Book of John, and I began by reviewing the first three chapters. Since we had visitors, I decided to read the first twelve verses of chapter one aloud:

In the beginning was the Word, and the Word was with God, and the Word was God. He was with God in the Beginning.

Through him all things were made; without him nothing was made that has been made. In him was life, and that life was the light of men. The light shines in the darkness, but the darkness has not understood it.

There came a man who was sent from God; his name was John. He came as a witness to testify concerning that light, so that through him all men might believe. He himself was not the light; he came only as a witness to the light. The true light that gives light to every man was coming into the world.

He was in the world, and though the world was made through him, the world did not recognize him. He came to that which was his own, but his own did not receive him. Yet to all who received him, to those who believed in his name, he gave the right to become children of God.

Then I asked some questions.

"What do we know about this 'Word' who created the world, turned the water into wine, and told a member of the ruling council that unless he was born again he could not see the kingdom of God?"

Betty, one of our regular members, raised her hand. "The fourteenth verse says, 'The Word became flesh and made his dwelling among us. . . .' Since the Word is God, we're talking about Jesus Christ here. The rest of the chapter makes that very clear."

"Thank you, Betty," I said. "It's extremely important that we understand this first chapter. I believe it's the answer to the cults that don't believe that Jesus is God in the flesh but merely a good man. A Jehovah's Witness told me once that Jesus was *a* god. This meant that she believes in several gods and that's idolatry." I got a little preachy and ended up saying, "If Jesus is God, we'd better listen to what he has to say and obey him."

That seemed to stimulate the discussion. We talked about how we could share with friends and neighbors who Jesus Christ is.

I was just about to close with prayer when Penny spoke up: "I told my husband that the Bible was true."

"I'm glad you were able to discuss that with him," I said. Then I gently turned the question back on her. "Tell me, Penny, do *you* believe the Bible is the Word of God?"

Her answer shook me to the core. "Shut up!" she muttered.

There was dead silence in the room, and I thought, *I must have asked the wrong question.* Finally, I gained my composure enough to say, "Let's just close in prayer."

I felt absolutely awful. Though I wanted to apologize to Penny for putting her on the spot, she was gone before I could reach her. I had been invited to a luncheon afterward but decided to call Penny as soon as I got home.

I arrived at my friend's home with a heavy heart. Serious concerns were running through my mind: *Penny will never come back to class. I've ruined everything. How could I have been so insensitive?*

Small tables had been set up for the luncheon, to which my friend had invited eleven guests. I looked across the room and there was Penny! When I learned she had been placed at my table, I prayed an S.O.S. *"Lord, I need wisdom."*

As soon as I sat down, I said, "Penny, I'm truly sorry I put you on the spot today. It was so insensitive of me. Will you forgive me?"

She apologized to me for her hostile reply. She had been flustered, she explained, by having her mother there. And she hadn't known the answer to my question. "I have a problem," she confided. "I don't know why I can't believe. I'd like to talk to you about it sometime."

"Why don't I stop over to your house next week and

we'll lay all your problems on the table and see if we can come up with some solutions."

"I'd like that. It's keeping me awake nights. I've got to settle this thing once and for all."

The following Saturday morning I had coffee at Penny's home. We talked in general terms for about an hour before she seemed settled enough to discuss the problem that concerned us both. "You told me the other day," I said, "that you were having difficulty believing. What exactly is hard for you to believe?"

"I struggled with my unbelief all during the week, but now I'm as ready as I'll ever be to accept Christ as my Savior." I could hardly believe what I was hearing. I had been prepared for some arguments, but Penny was full of surprises.

Then, rather shyly, she said, "All I need now is to have you pray with me."

I prayed and thanked God for the work of the Holy Spirit in Penny's heart in the past few days. Then Penny prayed and thanked him for sending his Son to die for her sin and for accepting her as his child. She ended with "Please help the rest of my family to believe in you, too."

There was a definite change in Penny's life after that. She told the class about the decision she had made and began entering into our discussions. She seemed very concerned about her family and friends. Her in-laws owned a family restaurant, and Penny invited the waitresses to attend our Bible study. Several were able to come, since Tuesday morning was not a busy time at work. Penny had a big station wagon and filled it to capacity. She brought as many as thirteen people at a time. It was great!

Tammy, her sister-in-law, had been attending for about

six weeks before she spoke up in class: "I've been feeling guilty coming to this class because I've always been taught that it was a sin to attend any other church but my own. But the memory verse for this week helped me to see that my former teaching has not been correct. You see, it says in 2 Timothy 3:16 that 'All Scripture is God-breathed and is useful for teaching, rebuking, correcting and training in righteousness.' What I'm learning here is Scripture, and it's good for me. I haven't learned that in my own church."

I love to watch the expression on the faces of the rest of the class when someone for the first time discovers the truth of God. Now everyone was grinning from ear to ear. They had been praying for these newcomers and were very interested in their responses.

After class, I asked Tammy if she could stay for a few minutes. Penny, who was driving, overheard my question. "No problem," she said. "Plenty of time." So Tammy and I had time for a little chat.

"Have you ever received Jesus Christ as your Savior?" I asked.

"But I'm not worthy," Tammy replied.

"None of us is worthy. There's nothing we can do to make ourselves worthy of the salvation Jesus came to give. He wants us to have it as a gift. Ephesians 2:8 and 9 says, 'For it is by grace you have been saved, through faith—and this not from yourselves, it is the gift of God—not by works, so that no one can boast.' "

This was new to Tammy, who had been trying to work for her salvation, yet had no peace.

"Would you like to receive this gift God offers you?" I asked her.

"Oh, yes. If it says that in the Bible, I believe it."

Tammy bowed her head and thanked God for the gift

he had offered her. "I now understand I can't work for it," she prayed, "so I'll accept Jesus Christ as my Savior and say thank you."

Soon after that, Tammy became concerned for her family, especially her son. After lengthy talks, prayers, and finding notes from her on his dresser, he too became a believer.

Penny and Tammy next became interested in getting the rest of their sisters and sisters-in-law to the Bible study. There was a problem, however, because some of them worked. Penny asked me, "Would you be willing to come one evening a week to teach a class at my sister-in-law Lillian's home? Everyone will be family except one—a close friend."

Even though it was a distance from my home, I was delighted for the opportunity. The first night, there were eight of us seated around a large table. They seemed excited to learn. Penny and Tammy had told them about the Book of John and that's what they wanted to study.

First we had an overview. Though their religious background had included some scriptural facts, none of them had read the Bible for themselves. As we went through John's Gospel over the next several weeks, I drew their attention to the many times Christ's enemies had sought to kill him. But "his time had not yet come," I read in John 8:20 (See also 2:4; 7:6, 8, 30.)

The women were fascinated. "Sounds like God really is in control of things," one of them said.

"Yes, God is certainly sovereign," I said. "His enemies couldn't take his life until he was ready to lay it down. It was for each one of us that Jesus died. He is waiting for our response to take him as our Savior."

"I'd like to," Sandy (Penny's sister-in-law) said, "but I wonder whether I will have this great emotional ex-

167

perience I hear people talk about. I read about Pat Boone and his wife. They were overwhelmed with emotion when they were converted."

"Some people do have a great emotional experience," I said, "and some don't. But, later, as they fully realize what Christ has saved them from, they have a gratitude to God that many times stirs them to the point of tears. To put the emotional experience first is like putting the cart before the horse, if you know what I mean."

I prayed for Sandy that week. I prayed that she would be convicted of sin and of her need for the Savior.

The following Thursday night we met again. I opened with prayer and then the flood gates opened. "I had my emotional experience," Sandy said. "It was awful. I feel like such a sinner. What can I do? I've got to get rid of this awful guilt."

"Sandy, that's why Jesus died. He took your guilt and now he offers you salvation as a gift. How about it? Are you ready to receive him as your Savior and Lord?"

I helped her pray the sinner's prayer. I thought, as we did it, that I heard another voice, faintly. When we finished, Peggy, who was the only non-relative there, said, "I prayed, too."

You should have heard the sounds of excitement! We were all so happy!

Then Peggy, with a smile coming through her tears, said, "There's another miracle that has occurred here tonight—something that you, Nellie, probably aren't aware of. But Sandy and I haven't spoken to each other for more than ten years, and tonight—at the same time—we prayed to God together to forgive us our sins and for Jesus to be our Savior. God took care of two things at once. Our neighbors will certainly be surprised," she added. "You see, we live across the street from each other."

## Reflection

It is not easy to know how far to probe in a class discussion. Sometimes it is better to approach a person on a one-on-one situation. We have to depend on the Spirit of God to lead us. Because of Penny's reaction to my direct approach I felt it was my fault.

I believe God allowed this incident to occur. That is evidenced by the results. We both apologized and became instant friends. The incident also opened the door for further opportunity to talk and resulted ultimately in her decision to accept Christ.

This total experience, which started with Penny, was almost like a replay of the incident in the first chapter of John, where Andrew found his brother Simon Peter, and told him, "We have found the Messiah." And Philip found Nathanael. Here, Penny brought Tammy, and Tammy brought her son to Christ, and then Sandy and Peggy came.

We need to be sensitive to the leading of the Holy Spirit, be willing to be his tool, and most of all desire to glorify God's name.

# 27

## What To Say When . . .

### She Says, "I Just Can't Understand a God Who Would Take an Innocent Child's Life"

**Barbara**

As she came to retrieve her tennis ball from our court, Barbara said, "If you ever need a substitute for a tennis game, I'd sure like to play. Maybe we could fill in for each other. How about it?" I didn't know her very well, but Barbara's doubles team had been playing on the court next to ours all season. We all agreed it would be fun subbing for each other. That way, we could get in a little extra tennis.

One day, while both of us were waiting for a court, Barb and I struck up a conversation. "I feel kinda blue today," she said. "Maybe I should say 'bitter.' "

"What's the matter?"

"I was thinking about my son. He was killed in an

automobile accident a few years ago and today would have been his birthday. He was only fifteen when he died. I've been wondering if I'll ever see him again." She turned away so I couldn't see her face. "Poor kid. He didn't even know his father, because my husband died when our son was only two-and-a-half years old."

"I'm so sorry," I said. "You've really gone through a lot, losing both a husband and a son."

"I just can't understand a God who would take an innocent child's life," she went on. "I never go to church any more, and I've lost all interest in religion."

"I'm sorry to hear that," I said. "When my youngest daughter came down with an incurable illness, I found that I needed God more than ever. Sickness, accidents, and other tragedies are all part of this life."

Before I could say another word, Barbara snapped, "I'm really not interested in religion, and I'd rather not talk about it." Then she brightened. "I am remarried, though, to a wonderful man. Cal and I have three children together. He's a Christian Scientist, but I don't buy that line."

We played tennis together from time to time, and neither of us referred to that conversation. I prayed for Barb whenever she came to mind but felt that since she had made it plain that she didn't want to hear what I had to say about God, it would be wrong to push.

One day I heard that Barbara had been operated on, and the doctor had found cancer. She seemed to recover quite well and was soon back playing tennis with an air of confidence, and certainly showing no sign of self-pity. I still was concerned but did not feel free to talk with her about the Lord.

About a year after Barb's surgery, my friend Marge called. "Barb's in the hospital again. She went in because

171

she's having a lot of pain. I'm afraid they've discovered more cancer."

For days I debated with myself about calling Barbara. I would wake up in the middle of the night, thinking about her. Then I would pray for wisdom and guidance as to what to do. Finally, since I couldn't get her out of my thoughts, I took this as from the Lord. After further prayer, I called her. "Do you remember the talk we had a couple of years ago?" I asked.

"I most certainly do."

"Barb," I said, "would you be willing to get together? I have something to share with you—something too good to keep to myself. Will you hear me out?"

"Well—"

"If, afterwards, you're not interested, I'll never broach the subject again."

She hesitated but finally consented to see me.

I went to her house, knowing she might be a little nervous. She was dealing with an emotional issue—her cancer; and I was dealing with an eternal issue—her salvation. I knew she would resist being pushed, so I started telling her about some of the troubled people I had met over the years. I told her how they came to Christ.

"I once met a woman, named Evelyn, in a swimming pool. She was there because of severe back damage. She confided in me that she felt her prayers hit the ceiling and that God didn't hear her. And, you know, Barb, Evelyn's problem was not only her back but a heart condition before God. She needed to come to God through Christ. As we sat by the pool, Evelyn prayed and confessed her sin of leaving Jesus Christ out of her life."

"Well," Barb admitted, "I'm just like Evelyn. You

might not believe it, but I've been trying to pray. But my prayers seem hollow and empty."

"Would you like to talk to God?" I asked.

"But I don't know how." She cried as tears ran down her face.

I helped Barb see that when she prayed, she could not bypass Jesus Christ, who had died on the cross for her sins. In order to get to God, she had to come through his Son Jesus. And she did!

"Lord Jesus," she prayed, "I confess my rejection of you. I need you and ask you to come into my life and to forgive my sins. Thank you for dying on the cross for me." When she looked up, a radiant smile broke through her tears.

Six months later, Barbara had finished four of a series of basic Bible-study books. She met other believers and enjoyed fellowship with them. Recently she came to visit and, while I was preparing some food, she remarked, "You know, Nellie, if I hadn't become ill with cancer, I probably would never have come to know the Lord."

Barbara and many friends prayed she would be restored to health.

"I want to live to honor the Lord," she said one day. "But if God doesn't choose to let me recover, I'm ready to do his will."

God did choose to take her home to be with himself. But through her death, her husband, Cal, came to know the Lord. I had the privilege of praying with Barb two hours before God called her home. It was at that time that Cal confessed his faith in Jesus Christ as his Savior.

I had just arrived home from the hospice when the phone rang. It was Cal's voice saying, "Barb's been healed at last. She's with her Maker."

## Reflection

Barbara had a real problem coping with the tragedy of her son's death. Job 5:7 is so true: "Yet man is born to trouble as surely as sparks fly upward." But the words of Jesus that Paul quotes in 2 Corinthians 12:9 are just as true: "My grace is sufficient for you, for my power is made perfect in weakness." What security we bring people when we tell them that neither they nor their loved ones will perish when they trust Christ as their personal Savior (John 3:16).

And, like Barbara, with some people you must simply wait and wait and wait until they are ready. With a cancer victim, it would seem to be natural to push, because we don't know how much time that person will have. But knowing *when* to present the cross will come as we ask and pray. Prayer is an essential part of evangelism. It is the cord that hooks us up to God's lifeline. Our part is to bring sinners into the immediate presence of the Savior—to bring them face to face with the Lord, so that he can press his claims on them and draw them to himself.

In John 12:32 the Lord Jesus said, "But I, when I am lifted up, will draw all men to myself." It is our business to tell others about him. It is his business to draw people to himself. It is only when we try to "touch the glory"— to put our own imprint on this holy transaction, to witness in the strength of our carnal religiosity—that things fall apart. Salvation is of the Lord. It is his, not ours.

We play our part by knowing the Lord and his Word, walking in obedience, praying faithfully, and speaking and acting in love.

Sometimes, when we are in the right place at the

right time, we may say scarcely a word and an unbeliever will believe. At other times, especially with relatives and close friends, we may be totally tongue-tied. There may be some people that we ourselves can never reach. Then we have to trust them to the Lord, who always has his "Apollos" (1 Cor. 3:6) to water the seed we have planted.

This realization takes the guilt out of evangelism "failures." Just because a person does not respond to our witness does not mean we have done something wrong (assuming that we've spoken in the Spirit). Guilt can cripple evangelists and stifle our witnessing. Refuse to let Satan batter your spirit with self-blame!

Witnessing is wonderful work! It is of the Lord. Rejoice in whatever little part he lets you play in leading someone to himself. Rejoice and be content.

# 28

## What To Say When . . .

### He Says, "I'm Beyond Redemption"

**Sam**

**M**ost of the people I pass on Ocean Boulevard are fast walkers. I try to walk fast, too. It's my daily health project. But Sam is a slow walker. He just trudges along. He never smiles or says, "Hello," but just looks down at the ground. Sam is quite a contrast to the rest of the walkers, all of whom are very friendly.

I had seen him several years in a row on my brief trips to Florida. One year we spent five months in Highland Beach because of my father's illness. It bothered me to pass this man, day after day, and not even get a smile from him when I passed.

I was able to get Sam's attention one day, though. I simply stopped and talked. "I've seen you walking down Ocean Boulevard for several years now," I said. "How far do you walk?"

"I walk seven miles every day, come rain or shine," he answered, with a note of pride in his voice. "It takes me all morning, but it gives me something to do."

"Do you have any other projects?"

"I play bridge with my friends a couple of times a week. I've done a lot of traveling, and I read a lot. Right now, I'm reading a book on the problems of apartheid in South Africa. I'm also into Dante, Virgil, and Homer."

"Have you ever read the Bible?" I asked Sam.

"Oh, yes, a couple of times."

"That's my favorite book," I said. "It has the answer to life. I read it every day, and it's always fresh and new. I find it very exciting."

"I can see that you do. But me, I'm beyond redemption."

"Why do you say that?"

"I just know I am."

"But God doesn't turn anyone away who truly seeks him," I prompted.

He laughed. "I have a friend who's a nun. She says she prays for me every day. If *she* can't convert me, I'm sure you can't."

"Only God can convert you, but I'll put you on my prayer list. I'll see you again. Bye-bye." And we walked off in opposite directions.

The next time I saw Sam, he actually smiled and greeted me.

"How are you coming along with your reading?" I asked.

"I'm still at it." He mentioned again the books he was reading.

"Have you read the Book of Romans in the Bible?" I asked.

177

"Probably, but I don't remember what it's about."

"How about reading the first two chapters? I'd be interested to know what you think."

"I'll have to finish my other reading first," he said.

A week passed before I was able to get back to my walking routine and see Sam again.

"Haven't seen you for a while," he said.

"My father is failing fast. My sister and my husband and I take turns caring for him. He wakes up at night, and one of us has to be there for him."

"I'm sorry about your father. Is he going to die?"

"I don't think he has very long in this life, but he wants to go home to be with the Lord. I heard him pray this the other day. He said, 'Oh, mighty God, have mercy on me, an old man, and take me home to be with you. I love you, Lord Jesus.' "

"Do you think God heard him?" Sam wondered.

"Oh, absolutely."

Then Sam said, "I've talked to leading theologians all over the world, and none of them can answer my questions."

"What is so hard that they can't answer?"

He looked at me with a condescending smile and said, "Lady, if theologians can't answer my questions, I don't think you can."

"Try me," I suggested.

"Okay. You tell me how God could hear *me* pray—I, who am just a speck among millions and millions of people. It's impossible and ridiculous to even imagine such a thing."

"Sam, you've told me that you do a lot of traveling and that you have friends in Europe that you keep in contact with. Have you ever talked to anyone overseas by phone?"

178

"Sure, lots of times."

"You mean to tell me," I continued, "that you can pick up an instrument, dial a few numbers, and talk to a person who is thousands of miles away in a matter of minutes? That's impossible and absolutely ridiculous!" I said with a bit of teasing in my voice. "Isn't God—who made us—greater than man?"

"Well, I suppose so."

"Think about it, Sam. By the way, my husband and I will be heading for Michigan shortly. Maybe, when we get back, you'll have had time to read the first two chapters of Romans—unless you're afraid to read them."

"I'm not afraid," he said.

"Okay, then prove it. I'll see you in about seven months."

He laughed and waved good-bye.

Seven months later, Sam was still walking Ocean Boulevard. He was friendly when we met, so I was surprised when he said, "I read the Book of Romans, but I don't want to talk about it."

"I'm disappointed," I said. "I was hoping we could have a good discussion." I thought perhaps he was disturbed by what he had read. But I was glad he had read it, since God's Word is powerful and will do its work in time.

The next few days, as I passed Sam, I smiled and greeted him but didn't stop to talk. Then, one morning, I saw him walking a couple of blocks ahead of me. Since he was a slow walker, it didn't take me long to catch up. He seemed happy to see me and became very talkative. He talked about the Iranian situation and how the press was trying to "crucify the President." Then he talked about taxes and stocks and bonds, and I found him very interesting and knowledgeable. I learned a lot.

Finally he got a bit agitated and said, "I'm a very prejudiced person. I can't help it. I'm really very prejudiced." He kept repeating himself.

"Are you prejudiced against the Jewish people, for example?" I asked.

He looked at me and laughed. "I'm a Jew myself, but I do think they are stupid at times. "Let me tell you what happened the other day, Nellie. I was playing bridge with my friends when they started to talk about former President Nixon. They tore him apart. They had nothing good to say about him and didn't give him credit for anything he had done. Then they started talking about King David, saying what a wonderful king he had been for Israel. They praised him to the skies. Now, how could they be so stupid? Why, David was a murderer. There's no comparison between what he did and Nixon's wrongdoings. I got up and left my friends. I couldn't stand hearing them talk."

"There's a difference though," I said. "You see, David repented. He was truly sorry for his sins. He actually agonized over them and everybody knew that. That's the difference. God knew his heart and forgave him. After that, David lived to honor God. In fact, God even called him a man after his own heart."

"How's David going to get punished for his sins?"

"David suffered remorse for his sin. He confessed his sin and was forgiven. You see, God looks at the attitude of our hearts. We can never fool him. You remember how in the Old Testament an animal had to be brought to the priest periodically as a sacrifice for the people's sin? The animal—a lamb or a ram—had to be perfect. The blood of the animal was sprinkled on the altar to make atonement for the Israelites. It was a covering for their sin."

"Yes, I know all about that," Sam agreed.

"The New Testament explains that Jesus Christ offered himself as a sacrifice for our sins. He was and is the Perfect Lamb who takes away our sin if we come to him and repent. Just as in the Old Testament the animal was the substitute for the sinner, so in the New Testament Jesus Christ is the substitute. The Bible says, 'He who knew no sin became sin for us.' "

"Jews don't sacrifice animals any more though," he said.

"I know. Jesus Christ was the final sacrifice. There's no need for any more sacrifices. He paid the ultimate price."

"Well, that's interesting. That's what you believe, huh?"

"Well, it's time for me to turn in," I said. "I enjoy these talks. Hope you do, too."

He smiled and continued his walk, and the next couple of days we just said "Hi" in passing. Then one morning, when I had reached the point where I turn around and walk back to my apartment, I heard a voice: "Wait and I'll walk with you." It was Sam. I was glad to see him.

"I have a present for you," I said, as I pulled from my shoulder bag a thin book called *The Reason Why*, by Robert A. Laidlaw. "With the way your mind works, I think you'll enjoy the way the author handles the arguments you come up with."

Sam seemed pleased and took the book. "Thanks. I'll read it."

Then he started to talk about taxes and investments. I listened and learned. At the same time, I waited for a crack to open in the door to his heart.

"My son is an attorney in New York," he said. "He's

181

in business for himself. I told him that if he wanted to make money, he needed to know that there is no right, no wrong, and no justice. You do what you have to, and you'll get along in this world. And, you know, he's doing just great."

"I can't buy that philosophy," I said. "My son is an attorney, too. He has a strong sense of right and wrong and also has compassion for people. He was once doing some legal work for a migrant worker in his area. He knew the man couldn't afford large legal fees, so he charged him one dollar. The man was grateful and Tim, my son, was glad to help a fellowman in need."

"That's not being a good American," Sam said.

"What do you mean?"

Sam laughed and said, "Haven't you heard the philosophy of the old West? 'Don't do unto others as you would want them to do to you.' " He admitted later that he was pulling my leg, and yet it appeared that he believed in looking out for Number One. "Now, here's something I've asked several people," he said, "but I'm not sure I've asked you. God is omnipotent. He knows everything, right?"

"That's right."

"God has also given man free will, right?"

"That's right," I agreed.

"Then how come he tempts people to do evil?"

"Yes, you've asked me that before. You must have forgotten my answer. You see, God doesn't tempt. Satan tempts. God tests. It's no different with your children. You would never tempt them or lure them to do evil. But you might *test* them to see if they can be trusted and if they've learned the things you've taught them".

"I see," Sam said, thoughtfully.

"By the way," I said, "you're talking about God. I thought you told me you were an atheist."

"No, I'm not an atheist. I believe in a supreme being."

"I'm glad for that," I said. "It makes as much sense to say there is no God or Creator as it does to say the watch you're wearing came into existence by itself."

"Yeah," Sam said.

I had found my talks with Sam very interesting. Three years earlier, he had told me twice as we were walking that he was an atheist. Yet, this day, he said he believed in a supreme being. I knew that God was working in him and that God was able to open Sam's heart.

Before he left, I said, "By the way, some time ago you told me you didn't mind going to hell because you would be with your friends. I thought I should tell you that the Bible says you would be cast into outer darkness and would not see your friends—ever."

"I don't believe the Bible."

I patted his arm and said teasingly, "Not yet, Sam."

He laughed as I turned to enter my apartment.

### Reflection

I will probably see Sam again and again if God spares us. My job is to be a faithful witness and to be available to the Lord. We have a great God who is in control of all things, but it was important that I have answers for Sam. It was important that I knew the Word of God and could remind him of the atonement from both Old and New Testaments.

Many people are afraid to witness because they know they will not have convincing answers for sharp unbelievers. But they have weapons the unsaved don't have. They have immediate access to God. They have the

Holy Spirit and the power of his might. And they can always say, "Hey, that's a good question. I don't know the answer one-two-three. But I'll research it and bring you the answer tomorrow."

As witnesses, we must be transparent, open, sensitive, responsive. The minute we give the impression that we are tricky, we lose our credibility and our opportunity to bring someone to Christ. Answer with Scripture whenever appropriate. To do that, you must be a steady memorizer. It is by knowing the Word that you can be instantly clothed in truth, whatever the season.

# 29

## What To Say When . . .

### *The Holy Spirit Has Already Worked*

**Suk Hun**

One day, Ken, our visitation pastor, introduced me to a very lovely Korean girl. "Myong Kim and her husband are visiting here from Boston," he said. "She attends Harvard and her husband attends M.I.T. They are both Christians. Myong would like to tell you about her parents, so I'll leave the two of you to get better acquainted." And he left.

"Pastor Ken told me you might be willing to help," she said. "My parents' family background is Buddhist. I became a Christian through my husband's family."

As we talked, I learned that Myong had been praying for her own parents for two years. Her heart's desire was that her whole family would come to know Jesus Christ as Savior and Lord.

"My parents are moving here from Korea. In fact, my

mother is in Korea now, finalizing the move to the United States. My father was president of a car company that is half-owned by General Motors. He will now work in this country. My mother will come to live near here next week, and I wondered if you would be willing to have tea with her. She would like to speak English better. She feels she could learn that best through conversation."

"I'd love to meet your mother," I said. "And I'll do what I can to help her."

Then Myong said shyly, "Do you suppose, as you get to know her better, that you could tell her about Jesus Christ? I've told her that I am now a Christian, but she needs to hear more." How I loved her for saying that! We both agreed to pray for wisdom, direction, and discernment.

Suk Hun, Myong's mother, was a most gracious lady, I found when I met her. Her Oriental manners were charming. As we talked and got acquainted, I told her about the Bible class I was leading. I asked her, "Would you be interested in attending the class? You would get to know some very nice ladies and also learn some things in the Bible and find out what Christianity is all about."

"I would like that very much, but I am not yet allowed to drive in America. You see, I have no license."

"I will be happy to pick you up," I said. And so I did. The time we spent in the car, Suk Hun and I, driving the twenty miles back and forth to the Bible class each week was most profitable. It gave us a chance to get to know each other's families and to contrast our values, our likes, and our dislikes.

Since several women in the class had not yet decided to receive the Savior, I made it a point each week to include God's plan of salvation and to emphasize how

186

to have a personal relationship with Jesus Christ. One day, as Suk Hun and I were driving home, she said, "I am very good student. I do everything you tell me. I study my lesson very good and read Bible every day."

Because of the language barrier and the fact that Christianity was so new to Suk Hun, I didn't try to push her for a decision. My thinking was line upon line, precept upon precept. I knew that as she studied, the Holy Spirit would use each line and precept to bring her to Christ. So I was very happy to hear her say she was doing her lessons. *Perhaps soon I can question her about her understanding of the gospel,* I thought.

Little did I realize that Suk Hun had been trying to tell me she had already received Christ as her Savior and only God. I later learned that it was Romans 8 that reached her heart.

She testified, "In Korea, I did not know who Jesus is. When I was in trouble, I would call out, 'Oh, God, help me.' But I did not know the Jesus God. No one ever told me about him. I did not know about the God who created the universe. But when I read in Romans 8:1 that 'Therefore there is now no condemnation for those who are in Christ Jesus,' I put my trust in him. Jesus has set me free from sin. I now belong to him. He is my only true and living God."

Every member of Suk Hun's family is now a Christian. Her husband was introduced to Christ by evangelist Billy Kim in Korea. Their youngest daughter, So Yong, was led to Christ through a classmate, and their son has also accepted Christ. They are a happy family who pray together and read the Bible daily.

Their daughter Myong encouraged them to attend Highland Park Baptist Church, the church where I am a member. They came regularly and grew as Christians.

All were baptized and have given a clear testimony of their saving faith in Jesus Christ.

One day Suk Hun said to me, "I remember that after I accepted Christ and heard Pastor Joe Stowell preach, I sat in my seat with my head in my hands and cried. I was so happy and had so much peace. I am so very thankful to my God, my only God."

The family now attend a Korean church in the area and are helping to make the gospel clear to their fellow worshipers.

## Reflection

Many people were involved in influencing this family toward Christ. The faithful prayers and concern of their daughter Myong brought out the truth of James 5:16b: "The prayer of a righteous man is powerful and effective."

This experience reinforced my growing conviction that God is continually at work in people's hearts. I had once thought I had to wait for the Spirit to work slowly, using each line and precept of the Word I presented. But he had been at work a long time in this woman's heart— without my help!

# 30

## What To Say When . . .

### Others Want to Know Him, Too

Witnessing is merely sowing the seed among people who want to know the Lord, and the opportunities for sharing the gospel are all around us. The secret is to be alert. Always remember: "The harvest is plentiful, but the workers are few . . . (Luke 10:2).

### Being Available

I never plan my witnessing experiences. They are spontaneous and spring naturally from encounters with people in all sorts of settings.

For example, in the past, when I went grocery shopping, I made a list and ran in and out of the store as fast as I could. Since I rarely like to waste time, grocery shopping seemed a necessary evil.

But when I became available to God, I decided I had better start noticing people and being a bit more friendly. So I began to talk. I would sometimes comment to people about their children. Now, on many occasions, I have said to a parent, "Isn't God good to allow us to have children? Quite a responsibility though, isn't it?"

I sometimes ask a child his or her name and hear "Mark" or "Peter" or "Debbie" or "Mary." (I never ask unless the parents are there, too.) I then tell the child, "I like that name. Did you know that's a Bible name?" This often gets me into a conversation with the parent.

Once I was standing at the meat counter waiting my turn when I noticed a little boy standing beside me. He was about five years old and had beautiful red hair. He looked up at me and smiled. Of course, I smiled back.

"Hi," I said, "I've got a nephew that looks a bit like you. He has red hair just like yours. His name is Joshua."

"Hey, that's my name, too."

"Well, now, that's quite a coincidence," I said. "He has a brother by the name of Caleb. You wouldn't have a brother by that name, would you?"

"Dad, Dad," he called. "Come here. This lady has a Joshua and a Caleb." His father came toward me and smiled a greeting.

"I take it you are Bible people with names like that," I said.

"We sure are," he said, and we had a good conversation right there. God gives us joys like that along the way if only we are willing to open our mouths.

I remember another time at the market, too. I had invited some missionaries to dinner and picked up a nice-looking roast from the display case. The label said, "English Roast." I turned to the woman standing next to me and said, "I've never bought this cut before. It looks pretty nice, but we've invited missionaries for Sunday dinner and I'd better be sure it's good."

"Oh, you'll love it," she said and even told me how to

prepare it. Then she surprised me by commenting, "You've got to be a Baptist. They're the only ones I know of who entertain missionaries."

We both laughed, and then she said more seriously, "I attend a church that as far as I'm concerned is dead. The minister doesn't give us teaching from the Bible. He just talks about current events and then gives us his opinion. Do you know much about the Bible?"

"I've had excellent biblical teaching both in my home and in my church," I said. "I've been encouraged to read it since I was a child. I try to read a portion every morning. It's a wonderful way to start the day."

We had a delightful talk, and I had a chance to tell her of the blessings of God's Word in my life—all over an "English Roast." I learned then that shopping is a good way to make connections. I just needed practice.

Another day, I was standing in line at the checkout counter at the grocery store. Actually, there was no line, I was the only customer. I noticed that the cashier wore a large cross on a chain around her neck. The cross must have been four inches long.

"My, that's an unusual looking cross," I commented. "Tell me, what does that cross mean to you?"

She took the cross gently in her hand, looked me in the eyes, and said softly, "This cross reminds me of the fact that Jesus Christ died on the cross for my sins."

"That's just great," I said. "I'm a believer, too."

Then the cashier looked wistful. "Before you came and while I was waiting for customers, I was praying for my children," she said. "Do you know what? You've made my day. I'm so glad you asked me about my cross."

That incident started me asking people about the crosses they wear. I get some interesting answers, like the one from a young man about nineteen who helped me put some peat moss in the trunk of our car. He was very friendly and we exchanged some words about the beautiful flowers at English Gardens. As we were about to leave, I said, "I notice you are wearing a gold cross. Tell me, what does that cross mean to you?"

He looked at me in surprise and said, "What do you mean?"

"Well, does the cross have any meaning to you?"

"I suppose it's a reminder of my religion."

"What does it remind you about your religion?"

"I really don't know," he admitted.

"Oh," I said. "I had hoped you would say, 'It's a reminder that Jesus Christ died on the cross for my sins—in my place."

"Say, now," he said, "that's really good. I hadn't thought about that."

I asked the same question of a clerk at the drugstore. Her answer was, "It doesn't mean anything except that it was a gift from my parents."

"Wearing a cross is an identity," I said. "It tells the world you identify with Jesus Christ."

"That never occurred to me. I'm going to give that some serious thought."

"Perhaps this booklet will help you understand more about who Jesus Christ is."

"Thank you very much," she said. "It was nice talking to you."

### Being Prepared

I have learned that another hindrance to witnessing is lack of preparation. I was picking up my friend at the airport when I saw some women sitting around a table on which was a sign that read, "Attend Our Christian

Seminar." It was being sponsored by a well-known denomination.

I walked up to one of the women and said, "I noticed your sign. What is the seminar about?"

"Let me give you some material," she said. "It will tell you."

"Can't *you* tell me about it?"

"You'll understand it better if you read this material."

Not getting any satisfaction, I then asked, "Can you tell me how I can become a Christian?"

"Not really," she said. "That's the job of the missionaries. They're downtown. I'll give you their phone number."

"Can't you tell me?" I persisted.

"Not really."

"Have you ever invited Jesus Christ into your heart to be your Savior and Lord? And are you a member of the family of God?" I asked.

"Oh, I did that some years ago."

"How did you do that?"

She hesitated. "Well, I prayed the sinner's prayer. I told God I knew I was a sinner and realized that Jesus died on the cross for my sins and asked him to come into my heart to cleanse and forgive me."

"Do you think he came into your life?"

"I know he did." She now spoke with boldness and excitement. "And do you know? This is the first time I've ever told anyone how I became a Christian."

"I'm so glad you did," I said. "I, too, am a believer in Christ and, as I understand the Scriptures, we members of the family of God are to pass the Good News on to others. It's not only the missionaries who have that privilege. We do, too."

"Thank you for talking to me today," she said. "You

really put me on the spot, but I needed it. I also need to be better prepared."

"Let me leave a couple of verses with you," I said. "In Matthew 10:32 Jesus says, 'Whoever acknowledges me before men, I will also acknowledge him before my Father in heaven.' And 1 Peter 3:15 tells us to always be prepared to give an answer to everyone who asks for the hope that we have."

Had I not confronted this woman as I did, perhaps she would not have become aware of her need to be prepared to give an answer to those who ask about her faith. But I did it in love, and that makes a big difference, since I didn't offend her.

### Following God's Leading

I have had other experiences where I have felt God nudge me to speak up. One happened while shopping at my favorite discount store. In the back room, they have designer clothes for 50 percent off or more, though they don't allow credit cards or returns. There are no individual dressing booths; everyone tries on the clothes in one large private room. I really don't mind, since there are lots of bargains and people will often strike up such interesting conversations that there's no telling what will happen.

I tried on a pleated skirt one day. It was beautiful and fit well. And the price? They were practically giving it away. A woman standing near me commented on it. "My, what a beautiful skirt. You ought to buy it. It's perfect for you."

"I like it, too," I said, "and I need something to wear to our midweek prayer service at the church."

"That would be fine to wear to prayer meeting," she said.

194

*She must be a Christian,* I thought, since she knew what a prayer meeting was.

"Do you ever attend prayer meetings?" I asked.

"I used to."

"You used to?" I knew I had a puzzled look on my face.

She was a bit hesitant to speak, but then she told me her story. "My husband was a pastor of a thriving Baptist church. People were being saved and the church was growing. Then my husband died suddenly. I had a very hard time and just couldn't face going back to that church. The people were kind and tried to comfort me. I know they tried to help, but I wouldn't respond. I was bitter and mad at God."

"Do you attend church at all?" I asked.

"Yes. I attend Unity."

"Unity!" I was flabbergasted. "Unity doesn't believe Jesus is God. They preach that we don't need a Savior. I'm sure you know better than that."

"If you want to know," she said, "I'm miserable. I would love to go back to my old church, but I'm embarrassed. What can I do?"

"That's not too difficult," I said. "First, confess your sin to God. First John 1:9 says that if you confess your sin, he'll forgive you. Then go to your friends and the church leaders. Tell them you've been wrong. Ask them to forgive you for your bad attitude. Tell them you've been mad at God for taking your husband. Be sure to tell them that you know it doesn't pay to be angry at God. It only makes you miserable."

"You know," she said, "I honestly believe that God sent you here to talk to me today. I feel so much better. I know now what I have to do."

Let me tell about another time when I overcame my

natural hesitation and spoke up in response to God's leading. Paul and I were playing tennis with a couple we met at the courts. We played every morning for almost a week. We noticed that Randy, the husband, criticized his wife every time she missed a shot. He would tell her what she did wrong. It didn't help her game. It just made her insecure and more inept.

Paul and I tried to encourage Ann, the wife, every time she made a good play. "Good shot" or "Excellent serve," we would say.

At the end of the week, Ann asked me, "Nellie, what makes you tick?" I was taken aback a bit and hesitated as I thought, *Do I dare tell her?*

I decided to let the chips fall where they may and answered, "If you really want to know, it's Jesus Christ."

To my surprise, she said, "Wow! Tell me about it."

While Paul and Randy stood talking together, Ann and I stood a little distance away. I had an opportunity to explain the gospel to her.

"I've heard this before," she said, "at a Christian Women's Club luncheon my friend invited me to. I'll have to think further about this way of life."

We didn't see the couple for a few days, and I wondered whether I might have offended Ann. About the middle of the following week, we met them on the court again. They seemed eager to play with us.

Ann came over to me and said, "I've been laid up for several days with a back problem. It wasn't so bad, because that gave me a chance to think about the things you told me. I discovered I had a great need to know Jesus Christ, and I want you to know I accepted him as my Savior. I've done a lot of praying these last few days."

Once again I was available for the Lord's work and spoke up. I'm glad I wasn't timid. Ann had a need, God brought us together, and I responded to her question. I must confess that I'm not always a model witness. Sometimes I may miss opportunities for witnessing. I was reminded of this the other day, when I had been timing myself to see how fast I could walk. As I passed people on the way, I would say, "Hello," or make some remark to let them know that I was racing against time. Ordinarily I would stop and talk, but not this day. I had forgotten that the Holy Spirit was running my life and that I had told the Lord I was always available to him.

It was the beautiful smile of the young mother, pushing her baby in a stroller, that finally caused me to stop and say, "My, what a beautiful baby you have. I've not seen you before. Do you live in the area?"

"No. We're just visiting my in-laws. It's such a beautiful day. I thought it would be good for the baby and me to get some Florida sunshine. We'll only be here for a week, so we want to make the most of it."

"I do hope you enjoy your visit. Your baby is so lovely. I hope you plan to bring her to Sunday school as she grows up and that, of course, you'll teach her about God."

Her answer came quickly as she gave me a big smile. "You bet I will," she said. "That's a top priority for me. And, do you know what? My in-laws are not Christians. I've been here for three days and I don't feel at home in a house where God isn't honored. This morning I prayed and asked God to please let me meet a Christian while I'm here. And here you are—the answer to my prayer. This is really exciting. God is so good."

This young mother, in Florida for a brief visit, was lonely for Christian fellowship—not lonely for someone her own age to talk to but lonely for another Christian. I was twice her age, but that mattered not. She was lonesome for family—real family—and Christians *are* real family. That day, we both learned the value of asking God to meet our needs and to help us be friendly to others for Christ's sake.

I believe we need to touch people for Christ every day—Christian and non-Christian alike. I know it pleases the Lord. But being friendly is only the beginning. Many people, even though they may have attended church, don't know much about the Bible. Others are new in the area and inviting them to a Bible study is a good way to get acquainted.

Betty had moved to Michigan from the East Coast. The adjustment was difficult for her, especially since her husband's job kept him away from home a great deal of the time. He was rarely available to help her with the many things that needed fixing in their new home. Betty was kept so busy that she had not had a chance to make new friendships.

She came to our Bible study at the invitation of a neighbor. Since the women in our group are very friendly, it didn't take long before Betty felt right at home. After attending the class for a few weeks, she remarked, "This Bible class has got to be the best thing going on in Michigan. I don't think I could have survived without it." Her enthusiasm never waned, and she was always prepared with her lessons.

I discovered that Betty's religious background was one of salvation by works. However, the Spirit of God used the Scriptures to turn her life around. One day I said to the class, "I'd be interested in knowing what portion or portions of Scripture have been the most help to you these past few months and why."

Without hesitation, Betty spoke up. "Romans 1:17—

'The righteous will live by faith.' And Ephesians 2:8 and 9—'for it is by grace you have been saved, through faith . . . not by works. . . .' These are my favorite verses," she said. "I no longer need to worry about the future. I'll trust God with my life. I can't work for my salvation. I've received it as a gift from God."

Betty glowed, and her firm conviction gave others the courage to share their verses. The love of Christ was truly in her life and she became a good role model for the rest of the class. We discovered that Betty had the gift of helps and was excellent at organization and encouragement. She was willing and able to plan and organize our year-end luncheon and worked well with others in this and other group projects.

She and I decided to do our marketing together on Fridays. The grocery bags were usually heavy, but I'm strong and never had problems with that. But one day Betty became very bossy and insisted on carrying them for me. I, in turn, insisted on carrying my own bags. "I may be older than you," I said, "but not too old to carry my own grocery bags."

"Oh, Nellie. There's so little I can do for you. Please let me do it for you. You've helped me so much. I'd like to serve you just a little."

When we got back to my house, once again Betty insisted on taking the groceries inside. It was then that I realized that her offer was an act of love—so I let her do it. We Christians always want to be the ones who give; but sometimes it's important that we be the ones who receive!

Once more let me say that I'm not a model witness. The first time I witnessed to a person about Christ, I felt tongue-tied. But as my dependence on the Holy Spirit grew, it became a thing of joy to me. The more I witnessed, the easier it became. This same principle has carried over into another area for me. With the Lord's leading, perhaps it will for you, too.

I had discipled Sharron for about a year before her husband was transferred to Ohio. I was delighted to hear later that both she and he had become active in a sound Bible-believing church and that they were growing in Christ.

One day Sharron called from Ohio and wanted to know if I would speak at a retreat their church was having.

"I'm not a speaker. I just disciple people," I said.

"Couldn't you tell the people what you've taught me?"

"Well, I suppose I could," I said. Though still hesitant, I consented to come.

Her church was about a three-and-a-half-hour drive from where we live in Michigan. Halfway there, I began to panic. Disturbing thoughts filled my mind: *You've got a lot of nerve. You're no speaker. How could you get yourself into such a situation?*

I began to pray: "Lord, please help me through just this one time. I promise I'll never accept a speaking engagement again."

When the time came for me to speak, I was still very nervous. But, at the same time, I had a deep trust that God would meet my need. I began to share my witnessing stories and how some of the people I had met came to know Christ. With growing confidence, I told each one detail by detail, just as I have here.

A woman came up to me afterward and said, "I'm just like the woman you told about who didn't know how to pray. I need Christ in my life."

Another woman came to me at church the next morning and said, "I prayed and invited Jesus Christ into

200

my life yesterday when you spoke." And Nancy, my friend Sharron's neighbor, accepted Christ.

As I drove home, I was ecstatic. I prayed, "Thank you, heavenly Father, for helping me and for blessing me so abundantly. It wasn't hard at all. In fact, if that is all there is to it, I'll speak any time."

And I've been speaking ever since, remembering that "a word aptly spoken is like apples of gold in settings of silver" (Prov. 25:11).

Words "aptly spoken" in witness to Christ bring people the message of eternal life. What a high value God places on such words! May we, each one, make ourselves available to him to use in this way.

### Reflection

Public speaking was new to me. The closer I got to my destination, the more I panicked. I even resorted to bargaining with God. Later, I realized how foolish I had been and I repented. God had said, "Be anxious for nothing" (Phil. 4:6).

Now as I end this book I can testify that God is faithful and his word is true. He used the seminar to nudge me to witness. When I first started to witness, I told him, "I want to be available to you. I don't know how to go about it, but please show me how."

Then, as the opportunities arose, God gave me another nudge. He brought the people and gave me the words to say.

Now I've told you my stories and I'm giving you a nudge. Tell the Lord you are available and let him answer your *"What Do You Say When?"* questions. Talk about the Lord and let him draw people to himself—through you.